WHITE RAINBOWS

Heal with Energy Medicine & Spiritual Development

SIBYL HARMONY

Sonoma Healing Press

With offices at
Sonoma, CA | Phoenix, AZ| | Nevada City, CA
Sonomahealingpress.com | info@sonomahealingpress.com

Copyright © 2021
Sibyl Harmony

All rights reserved. No part of this publication may be reproduced or transmitted in any form or by any means, electronic or mechanical, including photocopying, recording, or by an information storage and retrieval system, without permission in writing from the author.

Reviewers may quote brief passages. Thank you.

Print Book ISBN: 978-1-955897-02-0
Ebook ISBN: 978-1-955897-11-2

Library of Congress Cataloging-in-Publication Data available upon request.

Book Cover Typeset Fonts
Cinzel Decorative
Interior Typeset & Fonts
Candara
Cover Design – Shama Besley, Sonoma Healing Press
Printed in the United States

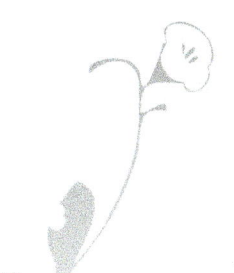

DEDICATIONS

This book is dedicated to all who chose to evolve.

And Prayers for those who chose not to.

To my Maggie and Dylan, the lights of my life.

ACKNOWLEDGMENTS

If you saw all the spiritual guides, and guardian angels, that walked through life with you, you would never again walk in fear.

Thank you, Robert W. for all the teachings.

Thanks to my sister Genie for putting up with me.

CONTENTS

Acknowledgments 5
Introduction 11
White Rainbows 15
Prayers & Meditation 19
    Prayer 19
    Meditation 21
    The Positive Effects of Meditation and Prayer 24
    Meditation-like Practices 25
    What you Resist Persists! 27
    Begin your Meditation Practice 29
Prayers 33
    Types of Prayers 34
Everything is Energy 40
    Your Spiritual "Energy" Anatomy 41
Aura 43
Sense your Aura Feeling Energy in Your Auric Body 47
    Cosmic Energy 47
    Earth Energy 48
    Grounding 49
    Grounding Cord 49
Chakras 53
    Your Chakra System 57
    Anatomy of a Chakra 57
    Individual Chakras 60
    Higher Self Chakras 68

Central Channel (Sushumna) 72
    Running Your Energy Exercise 76
The Clair Senses 79
    Clairalience (Clairescence or Clairolfaction) 90
Energetic Realms 94
Guides 96
    You Have Personal Guides 96
    Who is the Higher Self? 98
    James's story 101
    Remembering Childhood Guides 102
    Empower Yourself with Guides 105
    NOT MY GUIDE! 106
    David's story 107
    Spirit Guides 107
    Visualization for connecting with your guides 118
Our Inner Child 122
    Exercise to Heal Your Inner Child 124
    Hands on Healing Exercise 126
Divination 128
Healing or Balancing your Chakra 133
Healing with a Rose 137
Dreams 143
Summary 151
Appendices - Prayers 153
Dictionary of Symbols 160
    A 163
    B 172
    C 174
    D 175

E	....	176
F	....	177
H	....	180
J	....	181
M	....	181
N	....	190
P	....	191
S	....	193
T	....	193

About the Author 197
Work with Sibyl 198
    Book Private Sessions 198
    Workshops, Classes & Certificate Courses 198
Future Titles from Sibyl Harmony 199
Praise for Sibyl Harmony 201

INTRODUCTION

Part of my mission here on this planet is to help people heal themselves and others through Spiritual Understanding and Energy Medicine. White Rainbows will help you learn how to tune in with your own intuition and energy, so that through healing yourself you can download the energy that affects everyone around you and raises the vibration of Earth.

I always wanted to help the world be a better place, and I used to focus on changing outer circumstances and other people. But I found out the hard way, the only person and circumstance I really had control over was me and my own vibration. My job is to love and heal myself (my own energy). Everyone has "free will" and thus the clearest changes we can make are the changes we make within ourselves. This can be hard to do without tools or assistance as we are not "neutral" to ourselves and the energy we sit in. When we work with energy, we are able to uncover what we are unconscious to.

> *"Change you bless them."*
> *- My Guidance from Spirit*

In the time of the Goddess, Ancient Egypt, Atlantis, and Lemuria, we had knowledge and 12 strand DNA, and everyone was privy to their spiritual abilities and could create and manifest with our own energy. We fell asleep to those abilities due to certain humans trying to control the continued teaching of our own spiritual power by filtering what was taught as truth, using certain powers to control our awareness and consciousness. Now we are re-awakening to our spiritual truths. Those people and entities who are continuing to use energy to manipulate and control systems and consciousness, they will be seen for what they are. You will notice that anyone who is not working in alignment with the highest truth of spiritual freedom, the karma is showing up, and truth is being revealed.

This work is a gift, a tool the Ancients, and our Guides, and Teachers shared with all of us, and I am sharing with you. For anyone who uses these energy tools the agreement is that you will work with the highest standards and spiritual ethics, of self-healing, and re-aligning to our own Source Power and your own truth.

Energy Healing is a way to make the unseen seen or the unconscious conscious, to help you learn and more importantly remember who you are as an energetic being worthy of the unconditional love available to all of us. It is essential to answering the questions, "Why are we here?" and "What's my purpose?"

Energy healing has given me a depth of understanding and an additional set of practical "living" tools unlike any other that I can use in my daily life.

Traditional therapy helped by giving me a safe space to connect with my feelings and experiences. 12-Step programs were pivotal in saving my life and getting me sober. What these showed me, was that all the external people, places, and chemicals I was using to try to meet my needs weren't working for me. The one thing that was the common denominator was ME! Ultimately, it is my responsibility to come into my own power. To learn to work with my energy and go within and source the answers and solutions I need that will reflect my true self.

No one said it was going to be easy, but when working with spirit, I fully give my permission for its wisdom to ease my path.

My desire in this work is to give you the tools and support you need to develop a spiritual practice. One that will facilitate your own wisdom and help you feel confident in your ability to connect with your higher self, your guides, and the divine spark of spiritual intelligence that lives within you.

The examples, stories, and methods I share in this book will support you as you begin to practice and recognize your own spiritual experiences with energy medicine.

Thank you for giving me your time and love.

May we all be healed, because in truth we already are.

Sibyl Harmony

WHITE RAINBOWS

The ancient ones have said that rainbows are energetic "light bridges" that allow beings from other dimensions to travel to our world and bring divine healing, messages, teachings, and assistance to our planet.

In the spring of 2012, I was walking my dog in the hills near my home in California when a white golden arch appeared in the sky. *Can rainbows be white?* I asked myself. I was amazed, delighted, and surprised! *A White Rainbow how surreal.*

Because I've always been able to see energy, I wanted to double check to see if I was the only person witnessing this unusual display, so I asked other people who were walking by, "Do you see the white rainbow?"

"Yes! Isn't it amazing!"

Once home, I thought about the rainbows being light bridges and could only imagine what incredible messages Spiritual Travelers must have been gifting us across these light bridges.

The next day, the white rainbows were out again. My dog and I walked up the hill, today covered in a thick white fog. As we neared the top of the hill, the fog cleared, and my spiritual sight opened up. In front of me, standing next to a tree was this shining blue translucent figure of a man. Immediately I recognized his energy signature as the Ascended Master Melchizedek.

As a spiritual clairvoyant, I frequently see spiritual Masters, spirit beings, angels, and spheres of light from all religions. As a child, I would see and speak to the nature and tree spirits. Much of my training happens on the inner, and I work in the Temples of Isis and Mary Magdalena. My guides and spiritual teachers show themselves to me, illuminated by violet, pink, or blue light.

As we returned home, I could feel the presence of love all around me. Once home, I took the leash off my dog and couldn't wait to settle into meditation and ask if Melchizedek had a message for me. I've learned over the years that messages coming from spirit have many layers of meaning, none by accident. So, I knew this sighting was important for me to follow-up on. I went to my meditation chair, closed my eyes, cleared my energy, and invoked the presence of Melchizedek. As soon as I could feel the presence of love, I started to present my questions.

"Melchizedek, why where you up on the hill today? Do you have a message for me?"

Instantly I received a clear reply, "You are free to ascend."

In my mind, the message computed as, "I could leave this life now if I wanted to". I was being given the option to ascend out of this life.

My whole life flashed before my eyes.

I started to cry for myself. It's been such a long road. I had overcome so many obstacles. I started to cry for my loved ones, my friends, my students, and my family. I cried for the Earth, the people, the animals, the trees, and the oceans. I cried for us all. A deep healing cry, the kind of crying where your whole body is shaking and enveloped in grief and release.

Was I ready to die? Didn't I still have so much to do? I was really helping people. I was still learning so much. I had so much of my life's purpose yet to fulfill.

After taking the time I needed to process my options, I found peace in my heart and said, "Thank you so very much. I am so grateful for your love. But if it's ok, I'd like to stay here a little longer. I'd like to be of service to my students. I have children and grandchildren that need me as well. I can still make a difference here in others' lives."

I waited for several minutes and nothing happened, but I did get a sense that he was smiling at me, so I took that feeling as a *yes*, my request was received. I was allowed to stay.

The next day, my dog and I went for our walk along our usual path up the hill, and this time when we reached the top, out of nowhere, a young man dropped to the path. Startled, I thought *where did he come from, did he jump out of that tree?* He literally showed up right where I saw the spirit form of Melchizedek the day before. This man definitely wasn't a light being, he had long wavy disheveled brown hair, a beard, and was actively brushing himself off as he strolled down the hill. He was in a physical body.

As we passed each other our eyes met, he smiled warmly at me and said, "hello."

At that moment, I reflected upon the saying, "be careful when entertaining strangers, for you may be in the company of an angel". I smiled back, knowing that he was the physical confirmation of my experience with Melchizedek the day before.

In that same moment, I received a transmission for ALL of us "Earth Angels". "YOU ARE the Archangels, the Avatars, the Goddesses, and the Ascended Masters in the making."

To evolve and grow spiritually is our choice.

We have free will.

The God Spark and Divine Consciousness is within all of us.

These experiences have been part of my spiritual ascension here in the physical realm, the time of the white rainbows marked an important stage of spiritual initiation in my life and remain to this day a beloved symbol and gift I will cherish always. We are never alone.

PRAYERS & MEDITATION

Before enlightenment chop wood carry water.
After enlightenment chop wood carry water.

The language of prayer and meditation goes far beyond the image we have of the traditional, kneel down, bow our head, and ask for what we want, need, or hope for five minutes before bedtime; prayer is the act of communicating with spirit, God, Universe, or Source through everything we do.

I think of the practice of prayer as the request. I consider the practice of meditation as the listening. I then acknowledge and give spirit permission to animate and fill in the "how".

What we oftentimes don't realize is we are asking and communicating with the divine with every feeling, thought, and spoken word.

There is no separation between us and the Sacred.

Prayer

Many times, we limit ourselves and the potential for the miraculous divine results that prayer can bring, by trying to script it out, manipulate the conditions, or controlling how spirit (God, Goddess, Source) delivers upon our request.

Ask and it is given

When I was 34, before I learned about energy work and healing, I was diagnosed with Chronic Fatigue Syndrome. As many of you may have heard or experienced, this diagnosis has doctors completely stumped. After weeks of testing, the conclusion is, "There is nothing wrong with you." And you are sent home empty handed.

Literally having to crawl across my floor just to answer the phone, my body was wrecked, always exhausted and in pain and after months of no answers I felt completely hopeless and devastated. My outlook had become uncontrollably bleak.

At that time, I was in the early stages of developing a spiritual practice and I had opened myself up to the idea of prayer and meditation, and so of course, I would go through the motions and I thought I was doing my part. But as it is with most things, there was an evolution of learning I needed to experience for myself.

My basic practice consisted of five-minute meditations listening to a Shirley McClain Chakra Meditation CD in my chair. I knew something was happening even in that five-minutes, some kind of energy or changes were taking place because I would tear up from time to time. I couldn't at that time specifically identify what was happening, but I knew it was different!

Every day I would ask God (and anyone else who might be listening) "please restore me to health." I used to make this request every day for months, but nothing really changed the pain and exhaustion I was feeling.

But I stayed consistent. I wanted and needed better health. I knew the Divine was loving. What was missing?

Determined to get better, I tried a more forceful approach. I started taking control of my thinking: I needed to be more direct. One day I huffed out in utter frustration and desperation, "Fine, if this is going to be my life, I don't want to live like this!" My body instantly felt "icky", and I got the idea quickly that *maaayyybe that wasn't the best way to pray either.* With little to lose, I surrendered. I let go of my expectations about anything and offered my prayerful request one more time. "Just show me what to do, help me, guide me, I'm listening." It was only after that final shift in how I was asking, that I actually became open and aware to the information and people that were being guided to me. Within days I was receiving information about diet, vitamins, and nutrition. I transitioned to a super-clean diet and I was resting better, all of which was helpful and got me to a much better place, but I still hadn't healed.

This experience was the start of my true relationship with prayer (asking) and meditation (listening) that guided me to what I ultimately needed to learn; how to heal myself with energy.

Meditation

If one side of our divine communication is prayer, the act of asking or speaking to spirit, then the other side is meditation or the practice of listening to spirit and opening to the divine.

If, "everything is prayer" because we are always asking and receiving, so it is true, "everything can be a meditation".

There's some confusion in the ether about "meditation". Definitions can vary widely depending on who you talk to, and what their approach or spiritual training is. For me, meditation is a practice that can help us achieve states of listening, quiet, joy, healing, and peace. Most importantly, meditative practices strengthen our connection to our self, the world of spirit, and our higher intelligence helping us learn how to have a better relationship with our self, the world around us, and the divine. This way, we can receive the precious gift of knowing who we truly are and our soul's purpose.

Nowadays, it's nearly impossible to get away from the beeps, pings, buzzes, constant hustle and bustle and never-ending to-do-lists. Modern day life and expectations are bombarding our energy field at a rapidly increasing pace, external influences distract our thoughts, and unchecked ego turns us towards drama, anger, neediness, and fear. It's no wonder people find it difficult to find peace and true connection. Even sitting down for 10-minutes to clear your mind can feel overwhelming.

You can start anywhere with meditation.

Sometimes, meditation can be as simple as your body doing what it needs at that moment.

I remember years ago I was trying to meditate and thought I should be seeing angels, and getting prophetic messages, and images, and felt like I wasn't getting anything, I was failing at meditation.

Then one day, I started my practice as usual and for some reason my body began rocking back and forth. I thought to myself, *I hope no one is watching me, I probably look like a crazy person,* but suddenly, I found myself feeling more relaxed, less focused on what I was thinking and just in the moment being. *Ah-ha,* that is exactly what I needed. That simple unconscious movement helped to move my energy away from my mind and helped me to reduce the years of stress that had built up in my mind and body. The rocking was helping me achieve a state of relaxation which is what I needed to heal myself.

I've learned spirit always gives us exactly what we need, and we can trust that. Our job is to create the energetic space for the communication to come in and connection to be made.

Now I can meditate for several hours each day and I do see angels, guides, and get prophetic messages, but it took a devotion to my practice and a desire to heal.

Meditation is an important spiritual discipline and a devotional practice for me that I LOVE, I couldn't image my life without it, and wonder how I ever managed in my life before. I feel completely connected to bliss, the collective consciousness, spirit, and I can feel the unconditional healing love from the other side while in a physical body. I must admit I am always so amazed, surprised, and delighted, by the unconditional love, guidance and support that is there for me even if I don't always follow it, spirit is always there guiding me, and I am always learning. And for that, I am so grateful.

The Positive Effects of Meditation and Prayer

Imagine if we were to teach these simple and natural techniques to children. Imagine how much punishment and anger and perpetrating cycles of pain and crime could be avoided. Imagine how much less anxiety, depression, and medication would be in our societies.

Meditation teaches us to recognize, acknowledge, and respond to our emotion from a place of centeredness rather than reaction. The difference one minute of meditation can make has the potential to affect the balance between a good decision and a bad one. Over time, that one minute naturally increases as our human body begins to desire the state of peace and awareness it has come to rely on.

In Europe, these practices have already been implemented in schools as an alternative to punishment or detention, instead children are asked to first meditate and then speak about what they were feeling.

Meditation and prayer are responsible for some incredible things! Here is an incomplete list (feel free to add you own):

- Ability to heal the mind, body, and spirit.

- Slowing reducing the aging process.

- Opening up to wisdom that was previously inaccessible or obscured.

- Ability to be more present.

- Ability to know yourself better.

- Ability to connect with guides and the Divine.

- Ability to receive communication from the field.

- Awakening and elevation of consciousness.

- New ideas and inspirations.

- Facilitating inner peace and calmness.

- Experiencing greater alignment and harmony in your life and relationships.

- Being more aware and available to synchronistic events.

- Contributing to the greater good of the overall collective through the raising of your personal vibration.

- Healing trauma and releasing stress.

- Receiving a download of spiritual information and past lives.

- Develop psychic, mediumship, and channeling abilities.

- Connecting with your Higher Self, the Akashic Records and other realms of reality and wisdom.

- Teach children how to calm themselves and make good choices.

- Connecting children and adolescents to their purpose, joy, and creativity through helping them tune in more clearly to who they are and what they love.

Meditation-like Practices

There are many great meditation-like practices that don't involve just sitting still. I encourage my clients and students to try different types of practices that will relax the body, reduce mental stress, draw energy from the mind thus clearing and moving the energy which recharges the system and positively affects our spiritual anatomy.

Moving Meditation

Some practices have been specifically designed to move your physical body in order to shift energy and foster spiritual, mental, emotional, and physical wellness and connection:

- Yoga
- Tai chi
- Chi gong
- Sacred dance
- Spinning (Sufi)
- Indigenous prayer dances
- Mindful walking meditation

All of these are forms of mindful moving meditation that assist the energy through a specific set of movements to promote wellness and well being.

Other Types of Meditative-like Practices

A way you might connect with spirit is by doing whatever you love. When you are giving your energy to something you love you are open to your higher and creative self, more aligned to divine spirit, you will find yourself in "the zone" and might not even realize that you are experiencing a form of meditation, trance, divine interaction, and spiritual energy.

You may like walking in nature, you may be exercising, writing, playing music, chanting, drumming, dancing, breath work, cooking, giving to others, volunteering, making a home, fixing cars, gardening, creating art, spiritual study, skiing, surfing, swimming, camping, anything you derive pleasure from and can lose track of time doing because you are playing and working in the zone.

Meditation helps us to shift consciousness by focusing on our inner worlds as opposed trying to change or control our external circumstances. When we turn inwards, we have the ability to affect a change within us, that change opens the door for a shift to occur in our external reality.

As within, so without.

Even your work (believe it or not) when done with intention or heartfelt inquiry, can be a meditation, this helps you bring your awareness to the present moment, and this practice over time can help you shift your perspective.

What you Resist Persists!

I've always ended up living with people who don't wash dishes. I'd lecture on the importance of doing their own dishes. We sat through hour-long therapy sessions about why they couldn't wash dishes. We held long meetings. About. Doing. The. Dishes.

I became angry, resentful, and frustrated with these people. I had allowed their terrible lack of regard for me to knock me off balance, and as a joke – I even called myself "the dishwasher". Sometimes, I would get stubborn, just let the dishes pile up in the sink and surrounding countertops thinking, *Ha! that'll show em ...* but it didn't matter, I would eventually give in and do them anyway.

I fantasized about taking all the dishes outside and breaking every last dish and making everyone use paper plates. That never happened but I often fantasized about it.

Then one day – through circumstances and lives changing, I found myself living alone.

After a little while of flying solo, I realized – lots of those dishes were mine! So, not only did I now understand that I was not fully aware or present of what was bothering me at the time, I was also blaming the dishes and the people who I perceived as leaving them for me to clean, creating drama where there didn't need to be any and choosing to be in opposition, defiance, or resistance to what was.

With that realization, I decided to shift my consciousness and no longer resist the dishes. I quickly reached a place of neutrality, and eventually I started doing the dishes as a way to be in gratitude.

All those flat mates were excellent teachers. They taught me the valuable lesson of how to respect and treat myself, and that I can find peace, balance, and joy even while washing dirty dishes.

Before enlightenment wash dishes.
After enlightenment wash dishes.

Begin your Meditation Practice

Let's aim for a simple 20-minute meditation practice to start, which is what you need in order to re-set your energy field. Ideally, do this 20-minute meditation two times per day. If you meditate sitting upright in a chair or cross legged on the floor, you'll be less likely to fall asleep during your meditation. If you wish to fall asleep you can lay down on your back or support your head in the back of your chair, then start your meditation.

You'll find a 20-minute meditation is the equivalent of 2-hours of sleep. Because meditation restores and re-sets your energy. I would not recommend meditating after 6 pm as you may be unable to fall asleep until around midnight.

If you start meditating between 6 pm and 2 am you might end up not being able to fall asleep until around 2 am. If you wake up *after* 2 am, doing a meditation then can help you relax and fall back asleep because the natural bio-rhythm re-sets at 2 am.

Everyone is different, so you'll want to experiment and see what your body prefers, these are my most general helpful recommendations.

Prepare Your Space:

Before you begin your practice remember you are setting up sacred space to connect to your higher self, your guides and the Divine.

Find a quiet space (inside or outside), put your phone on Do Not Disturb or silence notifications, if you get cold you may want to get a blanket, have a pillow, a chair, or something to support your back, you might want to light a candle, diffuse essential oils, or read a quote from a book and set a timer for 20-minutes. If you find yourself wanting to look at the timer, it's best to only open one eye so that you stay in trance.

Invitation or Prayer:

Start by inviting or calling in your guides, angels, or spiritual advisors. You can start with something simple like:

> "I invoke my higher self and my guides to assist me and protect me during this meditation."

Or you can speak a prayer or a blessing, such as:

> "I invite my higher self and my spiritual guides and teachers to assist me and protect me and to bring healing and peace into my body, mind, and spirit."

Or you can chant gently a spiritual sound, or word that can help you stay in trance for example:

> "OMmmmmm" is a sacred sound and the Universal word for Oneness.

If you put music on – I recommend using sounds from nature such as forest or water, or you can use binaural beats that help you go into a trance state. I recommend not using anything with words at this point in your practice as this is great for when you are going on a journey.

Here we are simply invoking presence and relaxation to open us up so we can listen more fully to spirit. Trust that whatever needs to happen will happen naturally.

Your mind will want to grab onto things – when it happens, don't be surprised, just acknowledge it, and bring your awareness back to your sound, mantra, breath.

Begin your Meditation:

Close your eyes. You are now going into a bigger world … the world of spirit.

Slow your breathing … breathe in through your nose for three counts, hold your breath gently for two counts … and breathe out for two counts as you like.

Just let your mind focus on your breath … feel your breath traveling all the way to your belly … it's okay if your mind wanders … when you notice just come back to your breath.

Breathe.

Feel your body relaxing … feel yourself surrender to the peace, love, and stillness of the moment … you are surrounded by divine light … just keep your focus on your breath.

Whatever needs to happen will happen … just come back to your breath.

You are in sacred space … your body is healing on a deep level … you are connected to the quiet and the stillness … you feel the space within you expanding ever so slightly with each breath … Just keep breathing.

Come back gently before you open your eyes, let your spirit reanimate your body. Gently wiggle your fingers and toes. Take another big breath.

You might like to thank your higher self and your guides and speak that your meditation is complete.

Now open your eyes, have a stretch, and move your body.

To get the benefits of meditation your body needs to enter into the state daily. I recommend:

21-day Challenge to create a Meditation Practice:

- Set your timer, close your eyes, and meditate for 20- minutes every day.
- If you miss a day you need to start your 21-Days over again.

PRAYERS

Let's have a look at prayers and how they work. The Universe is always sending out a broadcast of love. When we speak a prayer into the Divine's or Source Creator's ear, it is a good idea to ask and then get out of the way. It's much better to say "this or something better" as this allows the Divine to bring answers and to work in ways that we haven't even thought of or couldn't imagine on our own. We can limit ourselves and our prayers by trying to give the divine orders and shopping lists. We might also consider the importance of listening as "divine guidance" is a form of answered prayers that can guide us to the assistance we need to co-create the manifestation we've been asking for.

It has been scientifically proven that when prayers are said for people they heal faster, and miraculous changes can happen.

All prayers are heard. Prayers are sent out on energetic waves of frequency and vibration. The universe and the soul respond when the energy of the prayer and their own conditions in this life or another time are met. Prayers might not be answered immediately as we cannot interfere with other people's "free will" and choices. We are all interacting with each other as individual soul's and we don't know what each soul is here to learn or experience. Therefore, a good prayer might be "bless them, change me." Rest assured when the time is right, and the energy of your prayer is a match for the soul or circumstance it will happen. Some prayers are instant because the conditions are right and are met with the supportive amplification of your prayer.

Miracles happen in accordance with divine time.

Types of Prayers

There are many ways to pray and many types of prayers. There are the prayers that come from urgency like "oh God please help me" a plea to the Creator for immediate relief. There are prayers of surrender "walk me through this, please hold my hand as I have no idea how I'm going to get through this" which allows you to put your life in Creator's hands. There's also the humorous kind, like the saying "there's no Atheist in a Foxhole" or the hangover prayer gripping the toilet for dear life "I promise I'll never drink again if you just get me through this misery".

There's traditional, affirmational, gratitude, land, and conversational prayers. We'll look at all of these below.

Traditional Prayers

I love some of the ancient traditional, well-known prayers such as the Saint Francis of Assisi. Some of these prayers resonate deeply for me as I might have recognized them from a previous life, and they hold a reverence that feels good in my soul.

Traditional prayers may be found in many ancient religions and cultures and some may be passed through your family lineage.

You'll recognize certain prayers in your life when you hear them or see them as good for you to practice. Not every prayer is necessary to know or practice. Always trust what feels right for you.

Daily Prayers

I do daily prayer before my feet even touch the ground in the morning. I do this so that I am setting the energy for the day and I ask to be in alignment, harmony, and balance with divine will and my purpose. "I call in my guides (by name, angels, ascended masters) hover over me. I will to be in alignment with the divine and guided in harmony, may I be of service, guided and protected, walk me through this day." And before I go to sleep, I always give thanks for this day "all that was given, and all that was taken away" and make sure I am connected to my guides in the dream world.

Speaking to the Divine – Conversational Prayer

One of the most direct and easy ways to pray is to simply open up and speak to the divine and your guides and angels as though you are having a conversation with your closest friend.

Affirmational Prayer

Is a prayer that is supportive of what you desire for yourself and your life such as "I am happy, healthy, and healed in this moment."

Gratitude Prayer

A prayer where you are giving thanks for your blessings. "Thank you for my health, my family, good relationships, this wonderful day, and the fresh air outside."

A lot of times prayer over meals or before we eat can help to affect the energy of the food we are about to ingest into our bodies by acknowledging the journey and the life that brought the food to our table.

We might give thanks to those who helped to seed, produce, and farm the land, and also for the animals or plant-life who are giving their life-force to nourish our bodies and to hold sacred space for those lands and all souls who gave their lives for us to be blessed. "Bless this food to my body. I pray for and thank the soul who gave their life, and the people who processed this food may they be safe and blessed, and may their lands, flocks, and farms be healed."

Prayer and the Land

When I'm in nature, I oftentimes receive messages from nature spirits and the old psychic and medicine people like the shamans do. Being in nature and being aware that there are plant, and animal spirits that guide our way and assist us in prayer is a powerful way to amplify and balance your energy while giving back to the land itself. "Bless this land that my feet walk upon, thank the trees for the air I breath and the earth for the nourishment I receive and bless all living things who dwell upon Mother Earth." You may also like to connect to the indigenous roots and original custodians of the land and thank them for their wisdom.

Celestial Prayers

We are of the Earth, but we are also of the stars. Praying to the stars is also a powerful way to manifest and connect to the beings of light in the heavens. "I invite the blessings and grace of my star family into my awareness and my life here on this planet. Thank you for attuning me to the cosmic cycles in the great beyond."

Water Prayers

Water is a conductor of spiritual energy and of all life on this planet. Water has been used as a purifying and life-giving agent in sacred ceremonies, anointment, and baptisms throughout time. Indigenous peoples would sing and dance as a way to pray and visualize rain coming to their lands. Sometimes, there is an overabundance of water in an area that may have experienced a flood or tidal wave and by invoking divine assistance through prayer it may help to rebalance the water.

Many of us also heal waterways and request divine assistance to help clear chemicals from water sources and to bring divine justice to industrial polluters.

You can also say a prayer to a glass of water you are drinking or bathing in as water can be influenced and structurally changed through thought and prayer.

The scientist, Dr. Masaru Emoto, conducted an experiment with more than 2000 people in Tokyo on the effects of positive and negative messages on water. Through a microscope the images of water crystals being affected by positive words completely healed and restricted the water crystal. A panel of 100 blind judges all came to the same conclusion of the water crystals that held a more perfected state of being through energy.

Prayers, Essences, Ceremony

Using sacred oils such as sandal wood, frankincense, myrrh, or other essences you feel connected to, can help purify energy and space and enhance your prayers.

Many cultures use plant medicine to burn and purify space during prayer and smudging ceremonies. Widely used plants are Sage (black/mugwort & white), Palo Santo, Cedar, Pine, and Eucalyptus branches.

Standing in a salt circle (you can use any type of salt) will help to amplify your prayers and protect you during prayer.

Prayer & Guides

We will discuss more about this later when we go into working with your guides, but I want to share that when you pray to or invite guides to support you, who you call upon and connect with is important.

A loving and protective guide or angel will give you a feeling of peace, love, and protection. Depending on your spiritual beliefs you might have a relationship with angels, Jesus, arch angels, Buddha, Hindu Gods, ascended Masters, Goddesses, and other spiritual guides who you trust. The key is making sure you pay attention to your feelings of safety, trust, and pure light.

If you experience anything else that is murky or ungrounded or invalidating, you can immediately disconnect from that guide simply by stating, "I'm not working with you." (read more about guides in our Guide section).

The Law of Attraction

Your thoughts and feelings are your prayers. Because the law of attraction is based upon the principle "like attracts like" and works through a system of frequency, vibration, and emotions that are all active in your energy field and act as the key to bringing the invisible into your physical reality.

In short, what I will teach you in my more advanced work is the energetics of matching and aligning your vibration to what you desire and how to identify what is active in your energy field.

Spirit knows your heart and your intention. Prayers and meditation create the foundation of preparing our energy for energy work, transformation, healing, and spiritual growth.

Prayers are powerful when they come from the heart. I have provided different examples of prayers that work for me in the appendices section in the back of this book. I invite you to use any that feel aligned for you.

EVERYTHING IS ENERGY

This a big concept, yet a relatively simple idea.

You are "Energy". You are spirit temporarily incarnate in a physical body. Your energy, your spirit is eternal, while your physical body is not.

When a person dies, the physical body stays behind on the Earth, yet the "Spirit" or "Energy" that animated their body has left.

Everything we interact with, eat, love, create is made up of energy and has its own vibrational field.

Human beings, the land, the water, buildings, plant life, animal life, insects, trees, stones, minerals, the stars are all energy and vibrating with their own unique energy signature that interact on different frequencies.

If we want to affect a change in our lives, health, prosperity, or relationships, first we need to understand the basic tenant that EVERYTHING, *and I do mean EVERTYHTHING… IS ENERGY!*

Your Spiritual "Energy" Anatomy

Your Spiritual Anatomy is the subtle energy body of your Spirit Body. It is your energetic makeup of your sacred energy that resides in and around your physical body.

In this section I'll teach you the foundations of the energy anatomy and how to use what you learn to heal yourself with energy medicine.

Your energy anatomy consists of:

- Top and Bottom Energy Ring that facilitates the flow of energy in and out of your aura.

- Your aura.

- Your Grounding Cord (feminine energy – Earth).

- Star/Cosmic Energy from Higher Source (masculine energy – Heavens/ Cosmos).

- The central channel that is where your soul is, top of the head to approximately the bottom of the tail bone (where the soul resides in your physical body).

- Chakras:

- You have seven main chakras.

- And many smaller chakras such as spleen, thymus, feet, and hand chakras.

- The higher self consists of the five chakras above your physical body.

- You have hundreds of smaller chakras (in all your joints, fingers, toes etc.).

Energy Anatomy Image

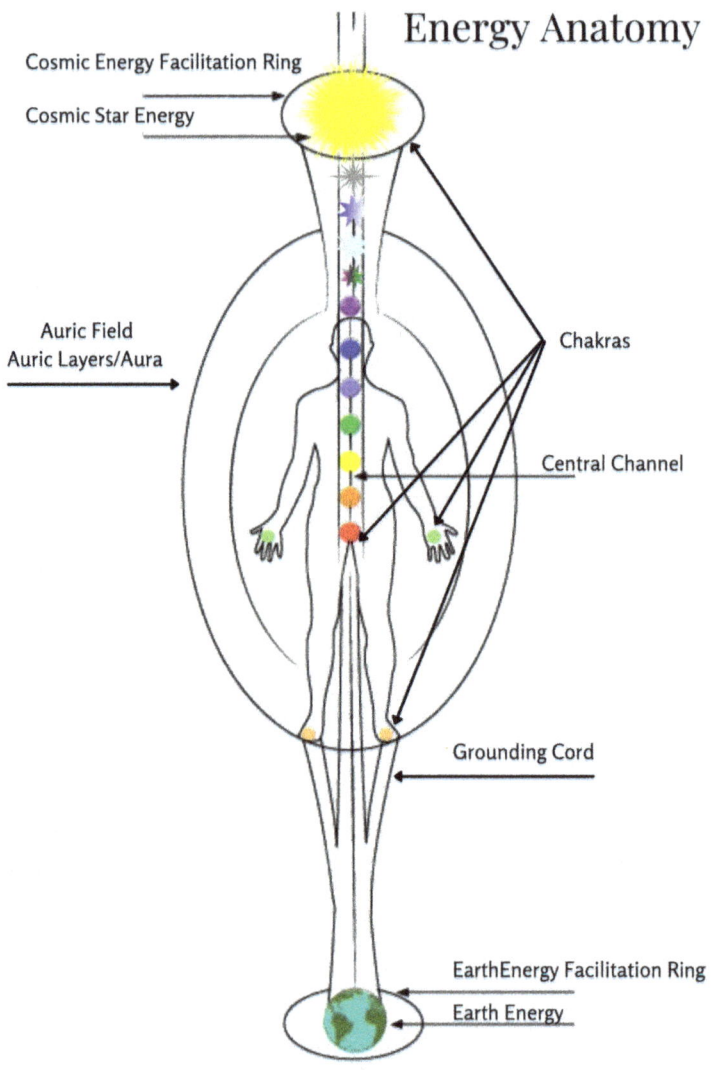

Aura

Your aura is light energy, every living thing on the planet has its own energetic aura.

The human aura, that surrounds the physical body is an egg like shape and has seven energetic layers.

The first layer of the aura is red in color, it extends about two to three inches from your physical body and permeates the physical body. This layer corresponds to your first chakra, and physical well-being.

The second layer of the aura is orange in color, it extends about three to four inches from the body and has to do with our emotions, it corresponds to the emotional body and the second chakra.

The third layer of the aura is yellow, it has an energy grid (imagine vertical and horizontal lines just like a grid), it has to do with our daily life, and corresponds to the third chakra.

The fourth layer of the aura is blue water, it has to do with feelings of universal love, compassion, and acceptance it corresponds to the fourth chakra.

The fifth layer of the aura is blue and white (like sky and clouds). It corresponds with telepathy, the intellect, and thoughts. It corresponds to the fifth chakra.

The sixth layer of the aura is rainbow colored ribbons. This is the layer where we connect with our guides, and it corresponds to the sixth chakra.

The seventh layer of the aura is golden sunlight and is our connection to Creator and our higher self. This layer corresponds to the seventh chakra.

A healthy aura is bright and clear with no damage. In energy medicine you can see and heal anything and repair the energetic damage that has happened within the aura.

If you have had abuse, illness, or accidents in your life, your aura may show what we call attachment cords, cracks, holes, dark or murky energy, or devices.

This is a picture of healthy aura.

The Aura

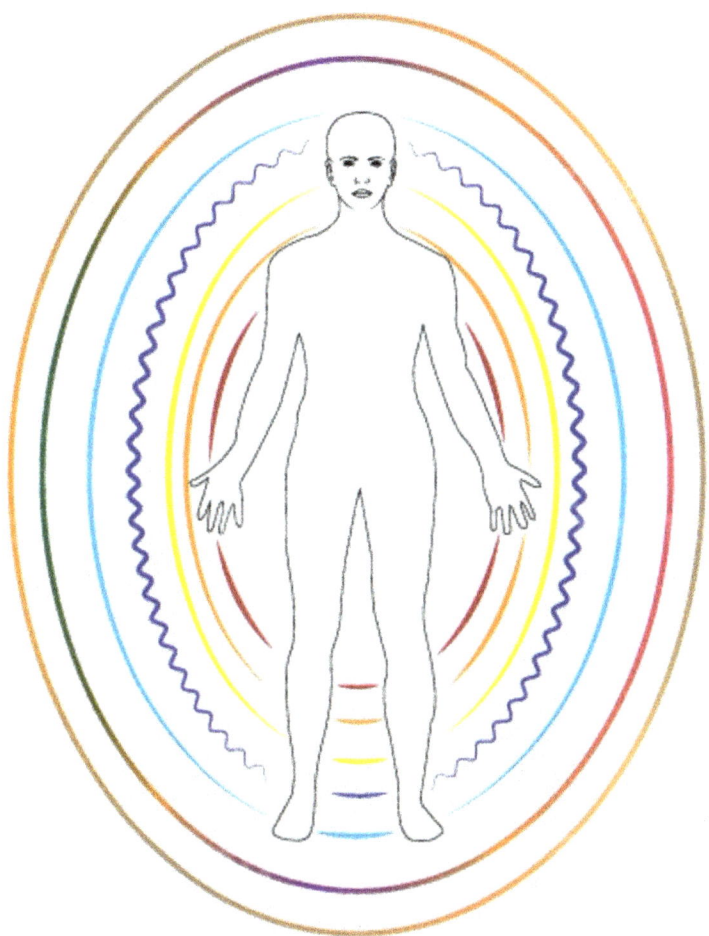

www.SibylHarmony.com

And below is a picture of a damaged aura.

Damaged Aura

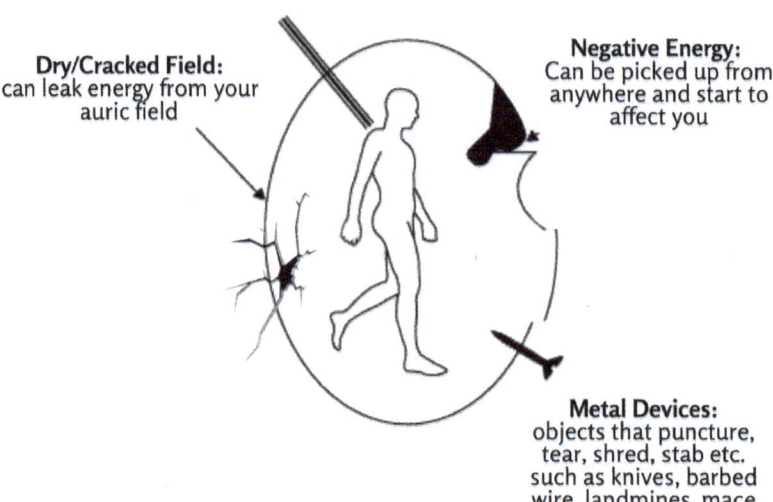

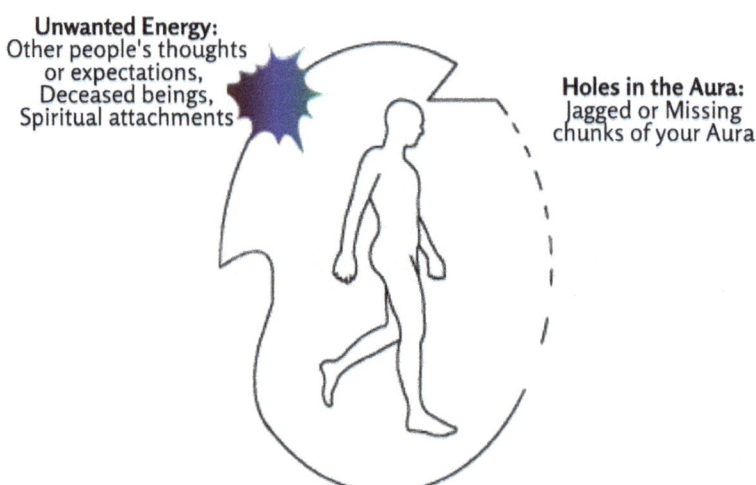

www.SibylHarmony.com

SENSE YOUR AURA
FEELING ENERGY IN YOUR AURIC BODY

With your eyes closed, place your hands about 12 inches apart, call in your guides, invite your higher self to sense your energy and slowly draw your hands together, notice when you start to feel the energy between your hands, tingling, magnetic, static, warm - you are feeling your energy field.

Just move your hands around different parts of your body and pay attention to what you sense, feel, or what impressions come up for you in your mind.

Cosmic Energy

Cosmic, Star, or Heavenly energy is the male or masculine vibration and manifestation energy. It represents "Father" energy.

The Cosmic energy comes into your body as a bright beam of light traveling through the five higher chakras into the top of your head continuing in a clockwise spiraling motion that illuminates all the chakras and activates your energy field. It is your connection to your "Higher Self".

Characteristics of balanced cosmic energy; protective, activating, approving, and illuminating, experiencing synchronicity.

Characteristics of unbalanced cosmic energy; you might not feel like you can connect easily to your higher self, or divine guidance. You can feel disconnected, blocked, confused, or unable to understand spiritual concepts or unwilling to connect with spirit, feeling out of time or out of place but can't put your finger on it.

Earth Energy

Earth, nature, or mother energy. Is the female or feminine vibration and manifestation energy.

The Earth energy exists as a ball of light and energy in the center of the planet (mother earth). When drawing Earth energy into your body it travels up through your grounding cord in a counterclockwise direction.

Characteristics of balanced Earth energy; healing, grounding, empowering, helps you to anchor your life-force into your physical body, own your space, and be in the present moment.

Characteristics of unbalanced Earth energy; health problems, not knowing who you are or what you want, ineffective, easily controlled or manipulated, lack of boundaries, lack of physical energy, can be easily knocked off balance, and accident prone.

Note: People who have had safe and loving childhoods, without illness or major trauma tend to be naturally more grounded and able to ground their energy more easily.

People who have experienced trauma, abuse, illness, body pain, or accidents tend to have a more difficult time grounding their energy.

Any energetic imbalance can be healed and corrected with awareness and practice of Grounding Techniques.

Grounding

Being "grounded" is extremely important to your physical health and mental and emotional well being on this planet. This basically translates into you being present in the moment of NOW.

It is important for you to feel safe in your body which is why learning about your energy anatomy and easy techniques to help you ground is our first stop along the energy anatomy map.

Let's look at how energy travels in and out of your body and how to have a grounded presence.

Grounding Cord

The grounding cord connects your life force to your physical body and the planet. It is your primary connection to the mother Earth female vibration that your body needs in order to be healthy and strong. Consider it your energetic umbilical cord to our collective Mother, Gaia.

How the Grounding Cord Works

The grounding cord brings energy up from the center of the planet into your body through your feet, legs, and tailbone in a counterclockwise spiraled motion (this is because the earth moves in a counterclockwise direction).

The energy of the Earth travels up the center of your grounding cord and connects you to the female energy of mother earth.

Released energy through your grounding cord travels along the outside of your grounding cord in a clockwise motion allowing the energy to be given back down into the earth (which she will intelligently utilize and recycle into what is needed).

The grounding cord can be as thin as 2-3 inches, or as wide as your hips (this can be a result of rebalancing, connection, or how much energy flow you are bringing in at any time).

You can expand or narrow your grounding cord and manage the energetic flow though it by using your intention and focusing on how you are connecting and circulating the inflow and outflow of your breath.

When a child is in utero, it is connected to the mother's energy. So, when the mother grounds herself, it automatically grounds and gives the child a sense of connection to the earth and safety up until the child is born. Children will unconsciously seek the feeling of safety through energetically grounding themselves by connecting a cord of energy to their parent's energy. If a child has had many earth lives on the planet before, they may have unconscious knowledge of how to ground their own energy at an earlier age (they might be "old Earth souls"). If a child has not incarnated often on this planet, they may need longer to feel safe and understand how to be here in a body.

At about age seven, children start to mimic other people around them, they now start to intuitively match and ground their own energy, they begin to feel safe, secure, and more independent in their own body.

Hint: When women are not grounded, they may feel angry with themselves. When men are not grounded, they may feel angry at women.

Your cord can become blocked, clogged, cracked, hardened, or weak, a reason for this could be if someone or something has taken up residence in your grounding cord and is causing you to feel less than connected or balanced.

Unless you have a young child, no one else's energy should be in your grounding cord.

Helpful Questions to find out if you are not grounded

- Are you easily knocked off balance physically and energetically?
- Do you feel energized in your body?
- Do you easily get distracted or off track, can't remember what you are meant to do, or why you walked into a room?
- Are you unable to focus on tasks?
- Do you have health problems?
- Do you feel anxious or unsafe?

Some Easy Ways to Help you Feel and Get Grounded

- Deep, slow, nasal, purposeful breathing.

- Stand on the Earth barefoot for as much time as you can, but after 20 minutes your energy will re-set.

- Give yourself a hug.

- Move or massage your physical body.

- Take a walk.

- Get outside in nature. Hug a tree.

- Holding, carrying, or wearing grounding crystals, such as: hematite, red jasper, obsidian, black tourmaline, or others.

- Eating or juicing root vegetables.

CHAKRAS

"Chakra" is an ancient Sanskrit word meaning "wheel of light". It is a center of consciousness that governs certain parts of the body and energy.

You have hundreds of smaller chakras in your body and twelve major chakras. First, you'll learn about the main seven chakras that are located in the body. Later in this chapter, you will learn about the five chakras above the head. You'll also learn about two smaller chakras I feel are important to mention which are the spleen and thymus chakras.

Believe it or not, you even have chakra centers in your joints such as fingers, knees, and elbows, at the tops of your feet and at the tips of your toes, in the palms of your hands and each finger. When a chakra is in good health the energy of that part of your body will function better and feel clearer.

You'll learn how the chakras work, how they are connected to your energy anatomy, and what each chakra governs physiologically and energetically.

Image a.

Side View of Chakras

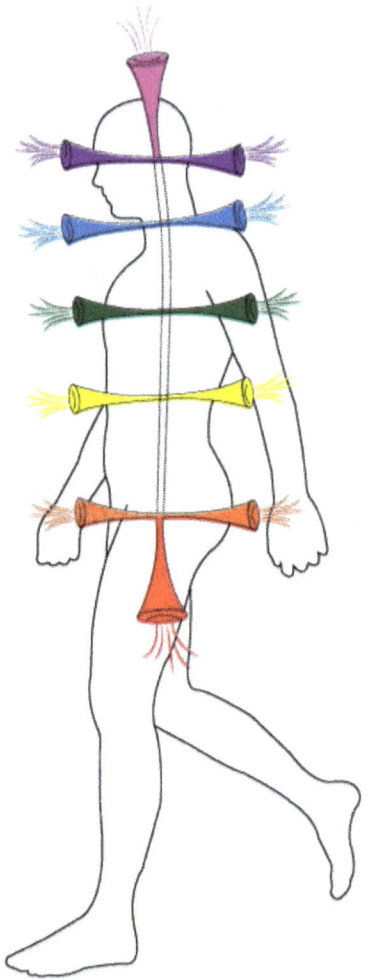

Side View Diagram of Chakras
Showing Energy & Possible Issues

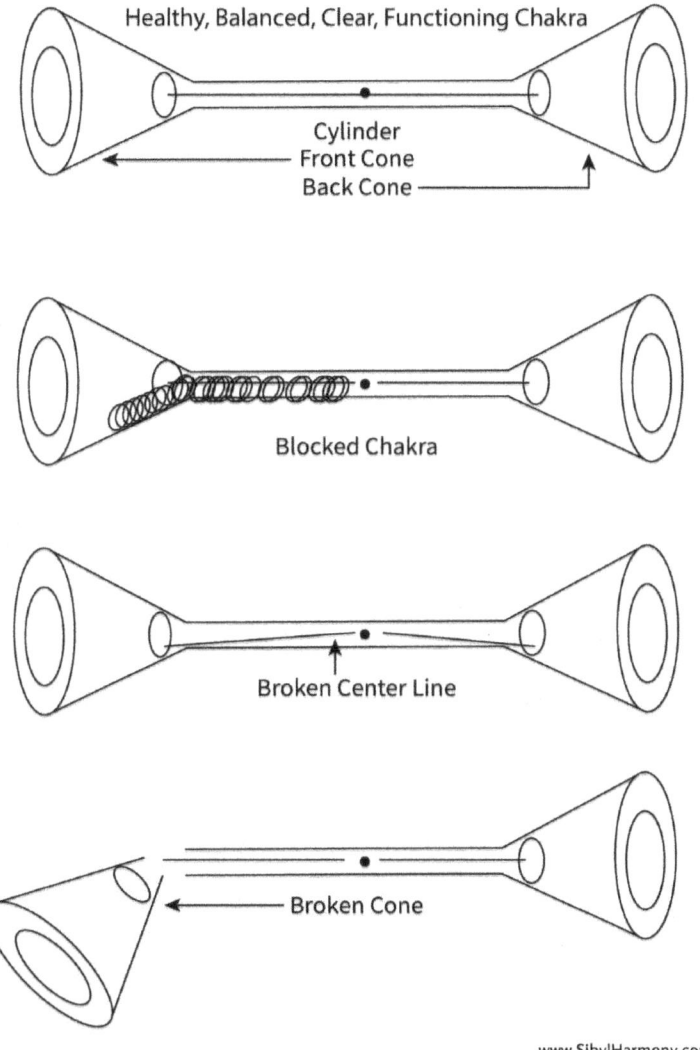

Front View of Chakra
showing the Moment of Now with clear energy

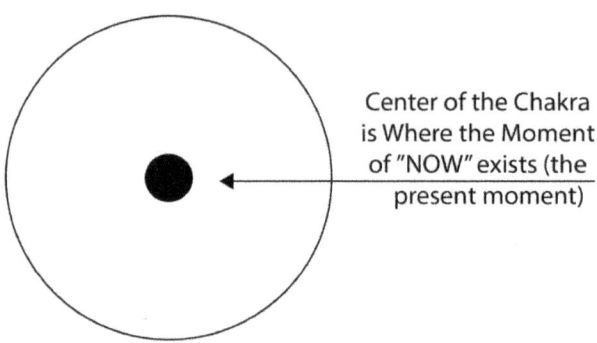

Front View of Chakra
with potential issues affecting the Moment of Now

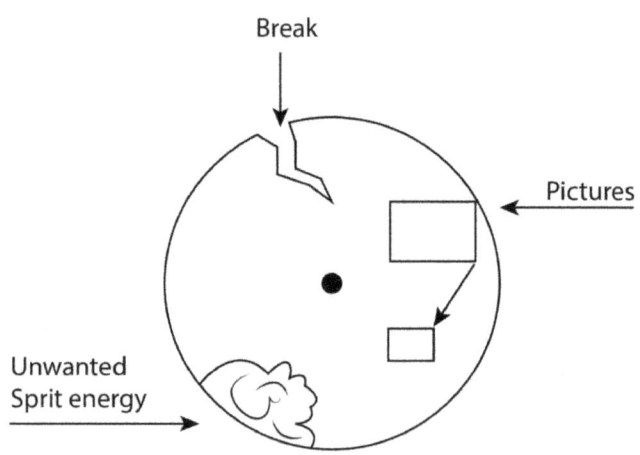

www.SibylHarmony.com

Your Chakra System

Your Chakra System is a subtle energy system, which means it's not seen with your physical eyes. However, you can see or sense it energetically. The importance of the chakra system cannot be understated because it affects every area of your life and houses consciousness.

Your chakra system is made up of hundreds of "cones" or "wheels" or "centers" of energy and light/life force. It governs your organs, energy, and important connections in your physical, emotional, and mental well-being.

Imagine this energetic record keeper that documents and records all the history of your current and past lives including: your feelings, thoughts, beliefs, relationships, prosperity, health, and spiritual growth.

I have found working with the chakra system specifically, to be one of the most effective approaches to healing source causes of dis-ease and illness and all states of consciousness.

In this book we will learn about 16 of the main chakras.

Anatomy of a Chakra

Each individual chakra, energy center, or wheel within the body is a cylinder with a cone that connects the front and back of the energy center with a line. As shown in **image a.** above the second through the sixth chakras share this design.

You will notice that the first and seventh chakras are different in their design being that they only have one cone. The first chakra cone faces down towards the earth and the seventh chakra cone faces up towards the stars.

The chakras that are in the energy field of the higher self, but not directly within the physical body are spherical or star shaped.

Side View of Crown & Root Chakra

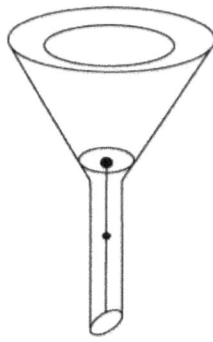

"1000 Petal Lotus"
Seventh Chakra, Crown
Facing upward towards the
Cosmos, Sky, Heavens

First Chakra, Root
Facing downward towards
the Earth

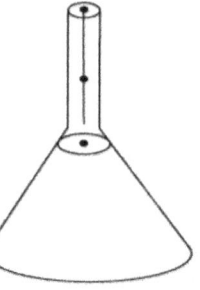

www.SibylHarmony.com

Diagram of Chakra System

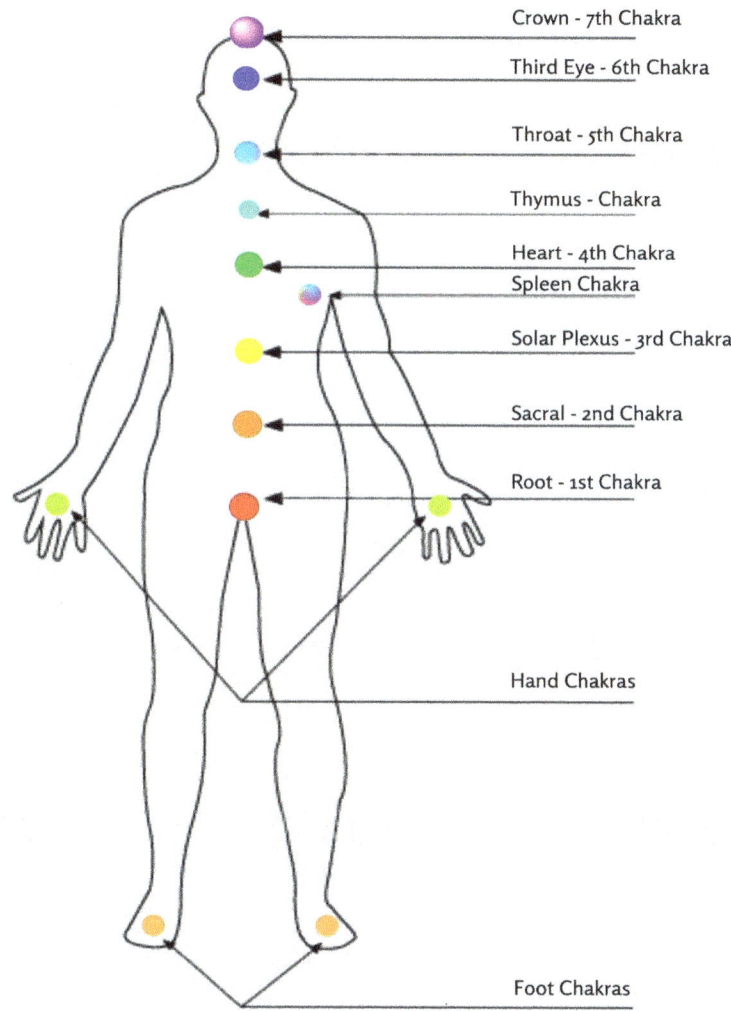

Individual Chakras

Each chakra governs states of consciousness and specific organs in your body.

First Chakra "I AM Response"

The first chakra (also known as the "root" chakra) is the most "physical" of the body chakras and rules instinct and embodiment. It is located in front of your tail bone and most of the time shows up energetically as the color red.

This center has to do with safety, home, and connection to family, society, community, groups, personal survival, and having enough. It facilitates grounding, getting things done in the physical world, and the physical act of procreation. It governs the colon, sexual organs, bones, muscles, blood, and adrenal glands.

Common feelings when balanced: the ability to respond to life rather than react, having enough, physical needs are met, being connected to community and family.

Common feelings when out of balance: anxiety, fears, stress, health issues, financial survival, instability, and lack. Afraid of not having enough, lack of abundance, being in "survival" mode (afraid of losing what you have).

Any abuse (especially physical or sexual), accidents, life threatening illness, or issues such as being forced to move homes too frequently, and the "fight or flight" response can be found in this energy center.

Second Chakra "I AM Amusement" (I AMUSE-ME-NOT)

This second chakra (also known as the "sacral" chakra) is the "creative" center of your body and rules your emotions, creativity, inner child, and intimacy. It is located just below your navel and most of the time shows up as the color orange.

This center has to do with the creative life force, new projects, new life, and "birthing" energy and governs the uterus, ovaries, testicles, kidneys, and bladder.

Common feelings when balanced: amusement, playful, comfort, creative, warm, romantic, expressive, healthy desire, trusting, in tune with your "clairsentience" (your "gut feeling" if something is right or not).

Common feelings when out of balance: fear, anger, revenge, jealously, addictions, overeating, drama, depression, fear of betrayal, deceit, and lack of trust.

Third Chakra "I AM Functional"

The third chakra (also known as the "Solar Plexus" chakra) has to do with our daily lives, general overall health, self-esteem, personal power, and personal will. This chakra, most of the time, shows up energetically as the color yellow.

Your third chakra governs the digestive organs, liver, gall bladder, pancreas, stomach, and small intestines.

Common feelings when balanced: radiant health, strong sense of self-esteem, balanced confidence, cooperation, team player, ability to proceed confidently.

Common feelings when out of balance: being controlled, controlling others, micro-managing, lack of personal power, low self-esteem, poor overall health, "my way or the highway", "kill or be killed", unable to move forward in life.

Spleen Chakra

The spleen chakra is on the side of your abdomen behind your stomach (not connected to the central channel) and is half the diameter of the other main body chakras and is a rainbow spectrum of color. When functioning and balanced it distributes its rainbow frequencies to other chakras and energizes them.

The spleen chakra governs the spleen and the lymphatic system.

When balanced: strong immune system, clean and clear headed, carefree, unconcerned, "no worries".

When unbalanced: low immunity, fatigue, stiff joints, a feeling of toxicity in your system.

Note: Too much sugar or worry can damage this chakra, one of the worst offenders is artificial sweeteners.

Fourth Chakra "I AM Joy"

The fourth chakra (also known as the "Heart" chakra) holds the consciousness of LOVE and rules our ability to love yourself and others.

It is located in the center of your chest and most of time shows up energetically as the color green.

This center has to do with unconditional love, compassion, and generosity. It governs the lungs, heart, and immune system.

Common feelings when balanced: joyful, content, open, at peace, caring, kind, warm, feel worthy of love, able to connect intimately, able to breathe deeply, capable of nurturing and caring for others, "others" centered vs. "self" centered.

Common feelings when out of balance: closed off, alone, apathetic, sad, lack of joy, fearful, shallow breath, cold, detached, unable to let someone into your heart or truly connect, co-dependent (looking for love or approval outside of yourself), you feel "unlovable", have blocked the ability to feel, unable to cry.

Thymus Chakra

This chakra is located in your chest between the heart and throat chakra. It is half the diameter of the other main chakras and shows up energetically as turquoise in color.

Some people call this the "higher heart". It governs the thymus which creates red and white blood cells that fight off infection and disease.

The thymus chakra works with issues of protection.

Common feelings when balanced: You feel protected, shielded, and strong.

Common feelings when out of balance: You may feel open to attack, unprotected, or weak.

Fifth Chakra "I AM Complete"

The fifth chakra (also known as the "Throat" chakra) is the center of communication, self-expression, and speaking your truth. It is located in your throat and connects to a network of smaller chakras that govern telepathic perception and communication. Most of time this chakra shows up energetically as aqua or sky blue color (with the smaller network of chakras appearing energetically as the color maroon). This center has to do with verbal communication, speaking in tongues, the written and spoken word, Gods word, judgment, integrity, common sense, and clear communication. This center governs the thyroid, sinus canals, teeth, ears, and connects to various release points around the face and head.

Common feelings when balanced: able to communicate clearly with honesty and integrity. We are less judgmental, more present in the moment and grounded in common sense, and more open and available to receive "clairaudient" messages and spiritual guidance. When you meditate and balance this chakra regularly your resonant voice (speaking and singing) becomes clearer, more rounded and fuller, and aligned to your authentic toning and harmony.

Common feelings when out of balance: low energy, sinus problems, teeth and dental issues, you might be lying more or out of your integrity, hiding something, or have a tendency or desire to argue. You might be draining others energy through an overactive throat chakra. You might experience a general inability to say or speak what you are thinking or feeling, a fear of speaking, feeling blocked, frustrated, unable to your find words, unable to communicate effectively, or articulate your thoughts clearly. You might also notice that you have a lot of mental "chatter" going on.

Verbal abuse from this life or another, negative self-talk, and channeling "lower" energies or vibrational entities can all be found in this energy center.

Sinus Chakras

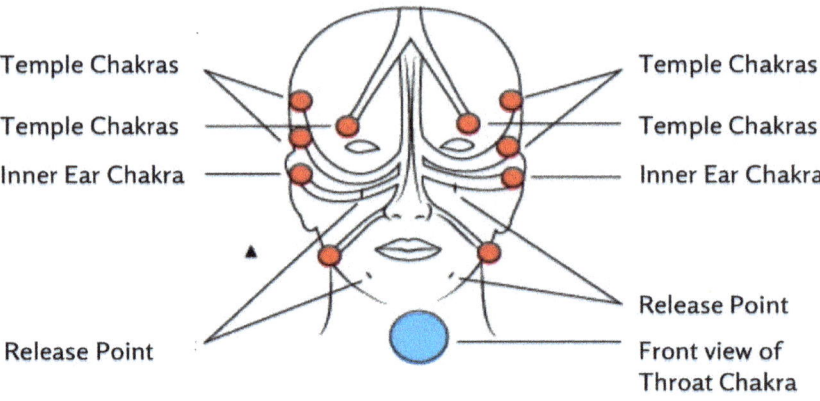

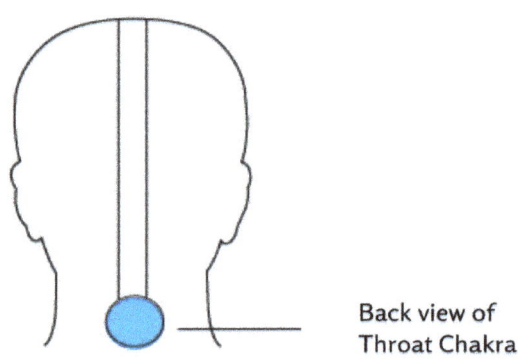

Sixth Chakra "I AM the Observer, I Understand"

The sixth chakra (also known as the "Third-eye" chakra) is the center of neutrality, spiritual vision, inner-knowing, wisdom, dreaming, prophetic visions, clairvoyance and being able to see energy and spirit. It is the place where we can look at ourselves and others "as the observer" from a more neutral perspective and is the starting point of being able see and access your higher self from within the body.

Most of time this chakra energetically shows up as an indigo blue color.

It governs your eyes, the hypothalamus, pineal, and pituitary glands (your hormone factory), it is also documented that the pineal is considered "the seat of your soul". When you sit in the consciousness of the sixth chakra, you can master your emotions from a place of neutrality.

Common feeling when balanced: you can see spirit and energy, experience peace and calm, your spiritual awareness feels activated and your third eye is open allowing you to receive guidance through visions and dreams.

Common feelings when out of balance: you may not be able to visualize, you struggle to remember your dreams, lack of awareness, over-reactiveness, hormonal imbalance, eye problems, or headaches.

Seventh Chakra "I AM Respect and Resolve"

This seventh chakra (also known as the "Crown" chakra) is also called the 1,000 Petal Lotus and is located at the top of your head. The color of this chakra usually presents energetically as violet and or gold. This is the beginning of our understanding, connection, and relationship with Source, Creator, God, Goddess, and our higher self. This chakra is the opening to the higher five chakras and states of consciousness that make up our higher self and reside outside of the physical body.

If an experienced healer scans the seventh chakra, they can find information for all the organs, intelligent systems, and subtle body energy. The reason a healer might not always start here with a scan is because they might receive an overabundance of information all at once. So many might be intuitively guided to start scanning or begin the healing and balancing at other chakras.

Common feelings when balanced: you might experience, peace, bliss, have glimpses of "enlightened" energy, and feel connected, filled, and guided by Divine Love. When you are aligned, clear, and balanced in your Crown - your direct connection to Source, Creator, God, Goddess, and higher self feels very strong. You will be able to easily download higher wisdom and knowledge "Claircognizance" and feel connected to light.

Common feelings when out of balance: feeling blocked from Source energy or your higher self, lack of knowing, unable to access higher ideas, or past life information. You may also feel you have a lack of freedom or choice in your life (freewill).

Higher Self Chakras

Eighth Chakra

This chakra is located approximately six-inches above the head and is violet, gold, and green in color (may be difficult to describe as they are spiritual colors). This is what many painters and artists have depicted as the "halo" that is seen around the head. It can also be seen as a sphere of light over the body. This is actually the golden light of the higher self radiating through the energy field.

The eighth chakra holds our past life information including soul agreements, karmic contracts, gifts, talents, and special training received (spiritual or other) in previous lives, and your desire to be of service (all found in the Akashic Records or "Soul Library").

Ninth Chakra

Appears energetically as a translucent white star. It carries Moon energy / vibration, "Divine Will", guiding your highest purpose, mastering your spiritual skills, and where you will meet your higher guides, ascended Masters, and the angelic realm. This is where you can channel healing light and the Christ consciousness.

The ninth chakra works as a team with the tenth chakra to create synchronistic events for your soul's Growth.

Tenth Chakra

The tenth chakra appears as a blue and gold star. This chakra is about bringing dreams into reality, and manifestation. Meditating on this center helps with "divine" or "spiritual timing" putting you "in the right place, at the right time".

This center is also where "Spiritual unconditional love" such as dolphins and pets are found (those beings who help and love us without any expectation).

Eleventh Chakra

This center may appear energetically as a silver star. This is the place where "devotion" dwells. Advanced healing skills and memory or the blueprint of these skills, higher purpose, service, devotion to Creator and Source, and your soul's path. This chakra is where you can develop and become "The Teacher", "The Beloved," "The Spiritual Master" through devotion.

Twelfth Chakra

Is gold sun. Connection to God or Goddess. Source. The Divine. Ascension divinity Universal unity. The *"Monadic chakra"*.

Thirteen and Beyond

Any chakras above the Twelfth level of Ascension you are leaving the Earth Realm and no longer working with "Earth Consciousness" or "Humanity". These are where souls will work with other dimensions, galaxies, and interplanetary beings, missions, or awareness.

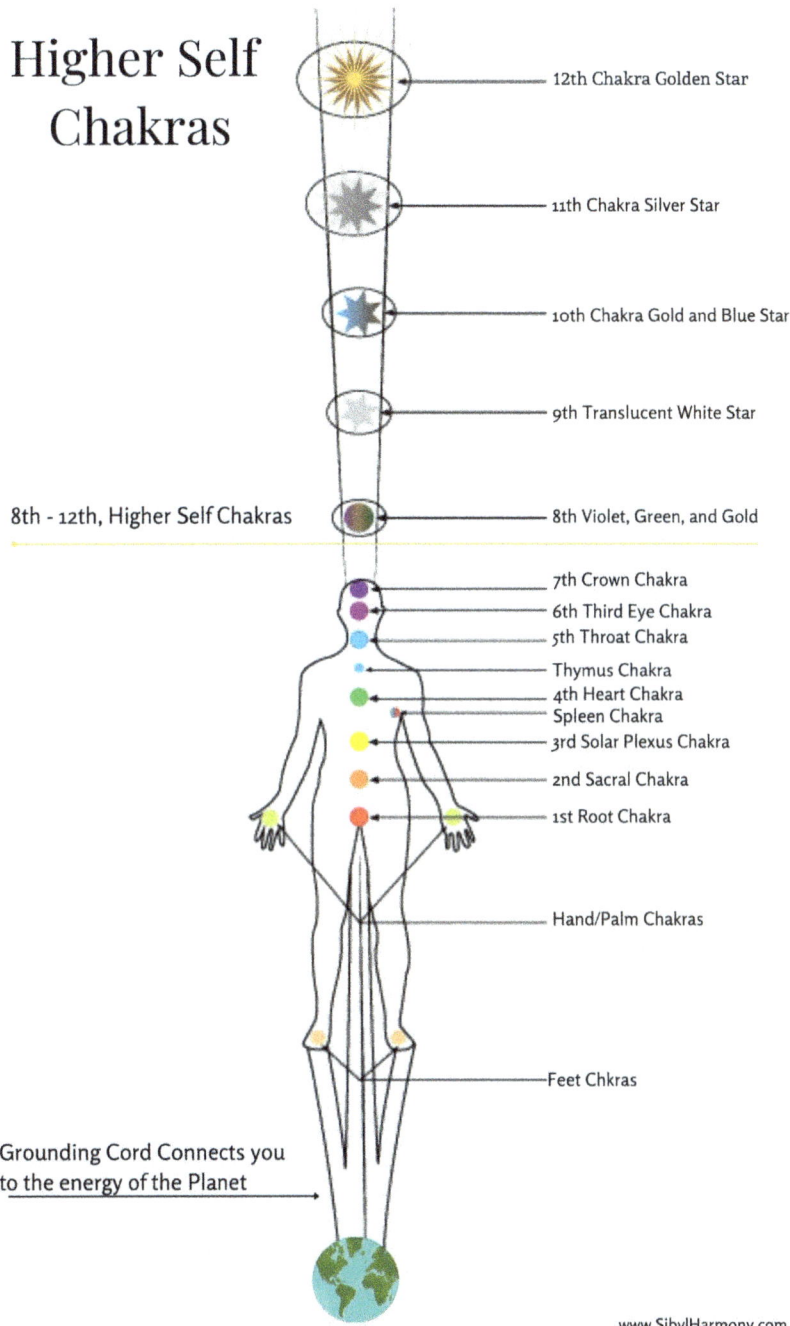

CENTRAL CHANNEL
(SUSHUMNA)

Sushumna is a Sanskrit word describing the energy that runs through the spinal cord, aka the central channel. This is the "Seat of your Soul" in your body. This channel is about 3 inches wide and runs from the top of your head to the base of your spine connecting all your chakras.

To heal the central channel, you can use the running energy exercise on the following pages to make sure that your earth and star energy is flowing properly.

Things that can be seen and healed in your chakras

Things that you might see causing problems in your chakras:

1. Pictures
2. Vectors, bug, spiders, snakes
3. Cords
4. Beings

5. Devices and implements

   6. Other junk, Karma and agreements

1. **Pictures**

Pictures can appear as a square if they are formed, they may also appear as bubbles if they aren't fully formed but in the process of forming and solidifying.

Pictures are beliefs, ideas, and events that have happened to you in this life or in a past life. For instance; you might have a heightened fear of spiders because you were attacked, bitten and killed in a past life and still carry the picture of that experience in this life.

These beliefs, experiences, or events can also be projected on to you from someone else and appear as a picture stuck in your chakra or energy field.

For example, let's say your father says "you aren't not good enough". Consciously or unconsciously some part of you believes him. He's basically just given you a "picture" of not being good enough. You now may carry this picture in your energy anatomy, and you might start to attract people, experiences, and events that mirror and match this belief or picture that isn't even yours. My goal is to help you discover this belief and others now so you can heal and release any illusions hidden and operating in your chakras and energy field. Pictures are beliefs that can affect every area of our lives. We live our lives through images and pictures, memories and feelings.

2. **Vectors**

In this category it is important to pay attention to how these actually show up in the chakra or energy field and how they "feel". Are they threatening, do they feel sickening, or antsy, or unclear. If so these are vectors.

Spider, snakes, bug, parasites, viruses (Creepy Crawlies that don't belong or feel good). These are different from animal totems where they represent power, healing, creativity and guidance. Vectors don't belong in your energy field.

Spiders cause actual physical pain and come in on the vibration of punishment. Snakes cause confusion, or fogginess of mind and decisions. Other bugs and creepy crawlies cause low energy and illness. The key is not to get freaked out, you see them now, so just to clear them.

3. Cords

Cords are different sizes. They can be small spaghetti strings or surgical tubing, or even larger. Whenever you are in relationship with someone a cord is formed. You are always corded to your parents and loved ones through cords of love. We're not looking for those kinds of cords here. Here we are looking for "discord" ,or disharmony, cords that draining your life force or sending you negative energy.

You can be corded to tragic or painful events, relationships, or emotions, such as an abusive or neglectful person or situation from this life or past life. You can also be corded to lower energies such as lower ego energies.

Not to worry, cords can be cut and cleared to end the connection.

4. **Beings**

The world and the universe is full of energy beings, they are mostly thought forms, or feelings. The may come across as depression, fear, or anger.

Psychic and shamanic healers, will see them as "beings".

In the upcoming exercise you'll be able to clear this energy.

5. **Devices and implements**

Devices appear as metal objects in your energy field that act as programming. For example: imagine a clock that the sets the timing and reaction for a specific emotion that behaves like a "landmine", it is set and gives you an automatic response that goes off like "clockwork". This is what we call a "devise". To heal from these automatic responses we need to clear the programming and removes the device. Devices may appear as a broken piece of metal, a tool, a metal instrument of some sort in your energy field or chakra.

Implements that are set up from some type or betrayal, or psychic attack (someone thinking negative thoughts about you or sending or wishing you negative energy) may come across in the form of an implement that might look like a dagger, an axe, a cleaver, or a sword, these can cause physical pain in your body (dull or sharp depending on the implement's energy signature or shape) or cause you physical discomfort or a feeling of being unwell.

6. **Junk and ending karma**

When doing healing you will see, feel, or know there is just "stuff and junk" that is coming out (like my technical term? ha ha.) It's just other unidentifiable stuff that doesn't belong there. You'll know this because the only energy that belongs in your body is your bright clear energy – anything else is showing up to be healed and cleared.

Running Your Energy Exercise

Find a quiet place to sit or stand (definitely don't do this while driving). Put a movie on for kids. Pets outside to play or take nap. Phone on airplane mode. You might want a blanket if you tend to get cold. I like breathing in essential oils or having crystals nearby that help with grounding. Obsidian, Hematite, and Black Tourmaline are great choices (or anything you are guided to).

Start with a prayer or affirmation like "help me to ground and run my energy, I call my energy back and surrender to the earth for peace and healing."

Take a deep, slow, and relaxing breath in through your nose and exhale however you like, connect your breath to the center of your head, focus in by placing a finger in between your eyes in the center of your brow, sense back three to four inches and that is where to connect your energy, the sacred space of your sixth chakra. Say "Hello" to yourself in the center of your head.

From the center of your head, drop a line of energy down the Central Channel (Sushumna) along the front of your spine and say "Hello" to the first chakra (root) and feel the energy at the base of your tailbone which is where you will sense your grounding cord.

Then say "Hello" to a safe place in the earth, imagine a place like an underground river, crystal beds, warm cave, or somewhere that feels good to you deep inside the planet and feel your energy travel down the cord to this safe place in the center of the earth.

Visualize or see a spherical ball of energy with a ring or halo of light around it. This sphere might be any bright, clear, warm, inviting, healing, energizing color that represents your energy in the center of the planet.

Feel the ring and halo of light as it facilitates the movement of energy from your sphere of light and travels up your grounding cord from the center of the Earth moving in a counterclockwise direction. The healing energy continues to move up the front of your spine and as you breathe it in it will allow the energy to flow easily and naturally into your body. Let it come up and flow out the top of your head infusing and circulating energy into you aura and chakras, where it needs to flow.

Feel the infusion come up through your feet and legs, bringing strength and healing. Sense energy branch from your neck area through your shoulders, arms, down your hand channels and fingertips.

Sense and feel the cycle of energy coming up the inside of your grounding cord and bringing life force from the center of the Earth through your higher chakras.

Now draw star energy into your body from the cosmos as it cycles back down through the top of your head in a clockwise motion, flushing and clearing away any blocks, debris, or sludge from your energy field and chakras that you are ready to let go of. Feel the old energy travel away from you down the outside of your grounding cord back into the planet earth where she can compost and transmute the energy.

Have fun, play, try things out, get creative, the more creative you are, the more you learn about how your body and senses work, the easier and more effective energy healing will be for you.

Most of the world is vibrating at serious and denser frequencies, in this exercise we are "un-matching" our vibration from the seriousness that is all around.

Try the intention to run the frequencies of joy, amusement, safety, peace, love, healing, presence, authenticity, and guidance. You can use this to set your energy for the day. Notice how you feel throughout the day, you might find that you are more of who you are or like to be, you might be more in balance and less reactive to circumstances or energies outside of you.

You can enjoy this for twenty minutes or more. As always, thank yourself for this sacred time and practice and have a beautiful day!

To listen to a guided version of this exercise with me, click the link below. See you there!

Click below to watch Running Your Energy Video!

https://sibylharmony.com/white-rainbow-videos

THE CLAIR SENSES

The Clair senses enable you to experience your intuition at a deeper level beyond what we perceive on the surface of life. The word "Clair" means "Clear", and these senses are oftentimes called "spiritual senses" or "psychic senses", as they allow one to receive messages and guidance from the "unseen" realms through the clear seeing, clear hearing, clear feeling, and clear knowing of information.

Every person is born with these "spiritual senses", some senses are naturally stronger or more prevalent than others and manifest differently for each person. When children are young, they are still very connected to the spirit realms and easily communicate and see beyond the veil. This "spiritual sight or hearing or knowing" usually starts to slow or shut down if the social or family consciousness doesn't know how to support keeping the connection open, or instills a sense of fear, or negative judgment around these abilities.

In this section you will learn what each clair sense is, how they may work for you, how to understand which of the senses are your strongest and how to develop the other senses.

As adults, many people have experienced glimpses of their gifts and have chosen to shut them down. This may be because of some feedback they've received in this life (from a parent, a pastor, a friend's family, or your peer group) that they were "different" or "weird" in some way. Perhaps you have trauma, memories, or contracts from a past life (for instance you may have perished in the Witch Trials, Inquisition, or were part of a mass wipe out of Indigenous Spirituality). These soul memories, historical events, and rigid belief systems may have come into this life with you, and they are already a part of the collective unconscious as humans on Earth. This karmic make-up signals to you that "it is not safe" to show your talents or gifts or to be different. When in truth these are our birthright, and they are empowering gifts that keep us safe and aligned.

When we are in tune with our clair senses, we are able to trust ourselves, have better boundaries, and are less likely to be controlled or manipulated by outside influences. Our clair senses play a much bigger role in knowing ourselves than "society" wants us to realize.

Everyone has some ability that can be cultivated. When you consciously use your abilities, they become stronger. It's like going to a gym and working out. We can build up your clair muscles and get you in great spiritual shape.

First, what are they?

How can you tune into these spiritual gifts?

Let's first talk about each sense and how it works.

Clairsentience

Clairsentience is the ability to "feel" spiritual energy clearly. The word sentience comes from the Latin root word sentire, to feel or to sense.

This clair is both physical and emotional energy. It is also the most reliable way to learn to trust your intuition through your feelings and is most closely connected to your second (Sacral) or third (Solar Plexus) chakra.

Your body is your biggest and best divination tool.

If this is one of your stronger senses you might notice the following: when meeting a person, you immediately tune in to how they *feel* to you, or how you feel around them. For instance, you might feel a sense of warmth, safety, joy, connection, or alternatively you might tune into a sense of negativity, or feel confused, unsafe, agitated, or a warning.

You might also be very sensitive to touch, texture, physical feedback. You might feel goosebumps, hairs raised, feel something brush your skin that isn't physically present, and highly sensitive to vibration.

Many people doubt in their abilities to connect with their spiritual senses, but we can all feel things.

Clairsentience is oftentimes more accurate than seeing a vision as there is a lot to consider when it comes to communicating and interpreting a vision. And many times, we need to go back and *feel* into the vision anyway. Developing and paying attention to how you are feeling, is one of the easiest and most powerful ways to start developing your other spiritual senses.

Trust yourself, listen to your body, and work with your clairsentience

One example I can share about this clair is when I was asked out on date by a tall, gorgeous man I'd been talking to for a while. Right before my first date with him I was getting ready and was doing some normal exercises to move my energy, all of a sudden, my back just gave out for no reason, and I had to cancel our date. My back took several days to heal. Later it was confirmed to me, it was not a good idea to move forward for various reasons. My body knew these things energetically before confirmation was possible, something was literally not in alignment for me in this relationship and my body stopped me from making this mistake by taking my back out of alignment. Now I'm grateful my body gave me such a clear signal, I'd had enough relationships that weren't balanced for me and my body, my clairsentience really could have saved me from entering another relationship that wouldn't have been great. Similarly, when we find someone and we feel alignment, balanced, easy, and supported, your body knows. Now I've learned to check-in with how I feel and how my body feels about ANY given situation, person, or event. It only takes a moment of pause. I'll teach you!

Key Takeaway: Your body knows – it is your biggest and best divination tool. Pause. Feel.

Easy clairsentience development practices: When something is good for me and my body it leans towards it, when it's not good for me I feel repelled, or like my body is leaning away.

You may start paying attention to simple movements like this, notice if you are being drawn to, or away from certain foods, herbs, supplements, people, areas, or how your body feels (energized, uplifted, supported, safe, calm, nauseous, headachy, stomach gas, confused etc).

Another way to practice and get to know this sense is by visiting different environments. Natural environments such as the ocean, desert, forest, plains all will feel different to you. You can also imagine them or get a photo from a magazine or online and gaze at the photo and just sense how it feels to you. Are you excited, can you feel yourself there, or do you lean back, does it go flat, or feel fearful, tight stomach, nauseous, or you immediately want to change the picture? This is the same with going on a vacation to an urban environment or a city or foreign land, use the travel brochures. ALWAYS go with your first feeling. Everything after that is your brain and not as reliable, as your logic will try to override your intuitive sense. Your "Clair" is immediate. So, practice that.

Ways to keep your clairsentient energy supported: take salt baths to clear your energy; use calming essential oils; treat yourself to a nurturing massage. Enjoy things that feel good to touch, soft and warm, or cool and refreshing, wear silk or soft natural fibers and enjoy the sensuality of texture against your skin. Wear colors that feel good to you and lift your vibration.

Clairvoyance

Clairvoyance is known as the sense of "Clear seeing".

Clair means "Clear" and "Voir" is French for "to look or see".

With this sense, you will have the ability to "see" energy and spirit clearly. It is most closely connected to the sixth (Third Eye) chakra right between your eyebrows on the bridge of your nose.

We are all clairvoyant because we see in our dreams with our third eye, and we can visualize things in meditation and contemplation or when we are engaging our creative imagination.

This may be one of your stronger senses if you receive messages from things around you that you can visually interpret as a "sign".

Bumper stickers, animals, shapes in the clouds, a flower, a bird, a photo repetitive messages like a clock frequently displaying the same time (11:11 or 4:44) when you look at it, or a butterfly that follows you down the street or hovers in front of your face. You might have been thinking about a question and you pass a bulletin board with an answer, these can all be the universe sending you "visual" messages.

Babies and animals have VERY STRONG clairvoyance, they have a natural connection to seeing energy, so pay attention to their reactions to things and to you!

You walk into a room and your vision is drawn to a book or picture; this can be another way spirit is directing you to a message that is for you. I can walk in a store and my eyes will go right to the foods or vitamins my body needs.

You may see flashes of light, orbs, or feathers on your path these are messages from your guides, angels, ascended Masters, or deceased loved ones that are making their presence known to you.

I mentioned earlier how I used to see and speak with nature spirits as a child. It was great because I had the space and time to enjoy these senses. As I got older, I started to speak with them less and have less time to give my attention to them as life got busier and more involved. So, I just didn't use this sense as much any longer. I was very sensitive and would get so much information I started drinking and using pills as a way to cope. This dulled my emotional sensitivity and dulled my clair senses. Anytime we are sensitive we have ways to develop or shut down. During this time of my life, I didn't know what else to do but to shut them down to function. This is where the techniques in this book can help you find ways to bridge your senses into your daily life.

Ways clairvoyance might show up: guides and spirits show up for me as a delightful show of colorful lights and orbs. Some people can see the aura and layers of color surrounding people, animals, plants, and environmental spaces. I see the chakras as I explained above, they appear to me very clearly in color. Or you may see full body aberrations of angels, guides, or who you were in a past life. I often see deceased people walking down streets or by the side of the road and in my sessions with students and clients where their guides, or family members have come in with them directly, or before the session in the dream state.

The thing I have found with clairvoyance is that I needed to use my other clair senses to decipher the visions and the beings, as it can be easy to misunderstand what you are seeing or why it is coming through. Don't worry if you haven't fully developed this clair sense yet, it can take time to trust what you are seeing and receiving.

Key Takeaway: If you ask, spirit will deliver visions or signs in your daily life and dreams. Pay attention to the simple things you might overlook, and where your eyes are being guided.

Easy clairvoyance development practices: Clairvoyance like all clairs can be developed by meditation and other spiritual practice. By breathing into your heart and feeling it open like the petals of the lotus, divine love will dissolve the scales of fear from your third eye so you can "see clearly".

You can experiment by creating a dictionary of symbols of what certain things mean to you, for example: seeing a bird – might be a message from spirit, a house – a symbol of the self, a car – might be a symbol for your "vehicle" or physical body, seeing a bee – might be time to get busy or a connection to ancient Egypt (symbolism is an art of your interpretation) have fun with it!

Ways to keep your clairvoyant energy supported: Clean up your diet, drink lots of water, meditate, and bring clearing light into your third eye and practice clearing visualizations, ask your guides and angels to be with you as you practice seeing and opening up.

If you have fear around seeing, or have seen lower vibration energies before – practice releasing the fear around using this sense. As I mentioned before, clairvoyant messages take time to decipher and can be scary at first as we don't know where they came from or what they meant. So, by inviting your body to reconcile the fear with love and protection you can start to open up to your messages and visions more fully.

Clairaudience

Clairaudience is the ability to hear spirit clearly through clear "communication". This sense is connected to the fifth (throat) chakra and the smaller chakras of the temple, ear, and brow. This sense is active when people are channeling spirit or "speaking" with spirit.

This might be one of your stronger senses if you pick up on words, and repetitive sounds or messages from your environments, the radio. Your inner ear plays a song from no-where that gets stuck in your head which is delivering a specific message to you or theme for your day. You might have exceptional hearing or pick up on specific parts of a conversation in the grocery store that answers a question you had or were thinking about. Also, when hearing a song on the radio you might get goosebumps and have an "ah ha" moment that you've just been given the answer or guidance.

You may also hear voices, or hear your name called or whispered when you wake up or when you need to pay attention. You might get an inner ringing or tone or violins or bells or whatever spirit is using to connect with you and get your attention and raise your vibration.

You may just hear words clearly, "yes" or "no" or "stop" or "turn" for immediate response. When your guides want you to research something, they might give you a riddle, a song, or a rhyme.

You might also receive messages telepathically – which instead of "hearing" actual words you might have "meaning" placed in your awareness, something you instantly understand. Beings from other realms and planets communicate this way and it is much more effective than using "lower language".

As you develop your fifth chakra, your voice will become more harmonious and resonant and improve your overall speaking and singing.

Key Takeaway: Sound, listening, and communicating with spirit. Experience "spoken word", "music", "channeling messages from spirit", and "speaking".

Easy clairaudience development practices:

Clear your fifth chakra, ear, sinus, and telepathic chakras.

You can experiment with ear candling, sinus flush, and meditation. Pay attention to your thoughts as those are "voices" in your head and learn to distinguish between your guidance, your guides and angels, and mental chatter.

Ways to keep your clairaudience energy supported:

Singing, chanting, prayers, activating your throat chakra, sound healing, singing bowls, chimes, bells, ting-shaw, gong, listening to resonant music and natural sounds.

Claircognizance

Claircognizance is the ability to know "clearly". Clair is "Clear" and from the root word "cognizant" which means "to know". This energy comes in through the top of the head which is the seventh (crown) chakra.

This spiritual sense is related to a strong knowingness and can present in thought or simply "just knowing" something.

This might be your stronger sense if you meet people for the first time, and you just "know" something about them that you would not have ever had the chance to learn. Or if you travel to a place and you have a "knowing" of where to go, or where things are, or what happened there this is one form of claircognizance. You might also have certain gifts and skills that you just "know how to do" that you were never taught, certain types of "genius".

You might also be able to easily "download" information or ideas instantly and clearly – you just "know" things that you otherwise wouldn't and haven't been "taught" (in this life).

You might be called a "know it all" by people because you kinda' are!

The difficult part of this gift is the trust factor – when you just "know" something, but you haven't "proven" it to yourself and others, it can be hard to trust this guidance.

There are three kinds of intelligences that are activated in the "mental" body – or "mind":

1. Cleverness – trickster, quick witted, mentally sharp, humorous, prankster, class clown, may use their intelligent abilities to manipulate, and may have a tendency to enjoy the energy of "getting one over" on something on someone.

2. Smart – Degrees, facts, figures, statistics, learnt and applied knowledge. This is higher "knowledge" that drives the researcher and teacher. This is a more analytical and theoretical mind.

3. Wisdom – this is when there is a higher, longer term knowing that leads to win-win and well-rounded solutions that serve everyone involved or even all of creation. This higher mind can be developed over lifetimes or can be channeled guidance from your higher self, Masters, angels, and guides. Wisdom is the highest form of claircognizance.

Key Takeaway: Trust your intuition, and the downloads, and guidance you receive.

Easy claircognizance development practices:

It is important for you to "follow-through" as a conscious practice on the downloads and guidance you receive. This helps you to develop greater "trust" in your "clear knowing" gifts.

Ways to keep your claircognizance energy supported:

Meditation, prayer, reading, study, and research are all ways to support, activate, and keep this sense open.

Clairalience (Clairescence or Clairolfaction)

Clairalience is the ability to smell spirit. It is not particularly common. Sometimes this is a key sense used in mediumship and connecting with deceased loved ones.

This might be a strong sense for you if you smell cigarette's when you aren't anywhere near a smoker or perfume. This might indicate you are picking up on the energy and scent of a deceased loved one who was a smoker or who loved that perfume.

Entities, attachments, and illness usually have a foul, stale, sour, or acrid smell associated with these lower vibrations.

Your guides and higher vibrational beings might have lighter or more pleasant smells, for instance the first time I smelled Jesus's Holy Aroma, it smelled like Frankincense and Myrrh. I recognize Mother Mary's presence as she smells like roses to me. When a place is energetically clean, or guides are around you may smell Lavender, Rosemary, Sandalwood, Roses, Vanilla, Sage, Citrus, Frankincense, Myrrh, or others.

Where I live, we've had severe fires, and many clients I work with might have experienced trauma during this time. If my guides want me to work with this trauma during a session, I will be able to smell the "fire" or "smoke".

Key Takeaway: You can receive spiritual information and know when Guides are present by paying attention to your "spiritual" smelling sense.

Easy clairalience development practices:

Tune in and practice if you notice different smells that have no other explanation. It is possible that this happens so just acknowledge it and then it will become more apparent.

Ways to support your clairalience energy:

Use a Neti Pot, meditate on clearing the fifth and the sinus chakras, make sure your area is clean of cooking odors or other smells that may interfere with you picking up spiritual smells. Avoid cigarette smoke or if you can, quit smoking. Try using 100% pure, uncut essential oils.

Clairgustance

Clairgustance is the ability to taste a substance without putting anything in one's mouth. This sense might be one of your stronger senses if you receive lots of taste information without having anything in your mouth.

This sense may also bring you information that tastes like a place, for instance, a forest or the ocean, this might be a spiritual message coming through from one of your guides or a late loved one who is connected this time place or space.

For me, this sense is activated by past lives. I came into this life with a wheat aversion and sensitivities, and during a past life regression session, I saw myself surrounded by large vats of wheat and baking every day. The taste of wheat was very pronounced in my mouth. So, this past experience energetically imprinted "wheat karma" into this incarnation to where I desired to not be inundated and overwhelmed with wheat. So, I balanced my experience with wheat, by having an aversion to wheat in my body during this life.

When we receive this kind of information it can all be cleared and healed because we now have an awareness of where to look and where it comes from.

Key Takeaway: Taste is a very strong indicator of mediumship abilities, past life connections, and spiritual communications.

Easy ways to develop your clairgustance sense:

In meditation, think about your relationship with taste. Ask for spirit to bring forth a taste in your mouth if it is important for you.

Keep a dream journal and notice any tastes that you are getting in your dreams or wake up with in your mouth. Write down any feelings or visions that arise with random tastes.

Ways to keep your clairgustance energy supported:

Stay hydrated so your tastes can communicate clearly and pay attention the tastes that you receive that have no physical source.

What's Next

Everyone has clair senses, and you can strengthen and develop your senses through the practices I give you in my books, classes, and in meditation.

ENERGETIC REALMS

Every soul has an "origin story" and is connected to different Realms or "groups" of existence. Your soul might have come from the Elemental Realm (fairies, leprechauns, nature spirits, mermaids, dragons, animal spirits, and indigenous cultures), the Angelic Realm (angels and souls that haven't incarnated as much in the Earth Realm), the Cosmic and Star Seed Realms (extraterrestrial and other star system knowledge and connection), Ascended Masters (old souls that have incarnated many times in the Earth Plane and are familiar with human nature, the Wise Ones).

The energetic realms your soul comes from can determine what kind of guides you have and connect with most easily.

It is possible (or even likely) that you are a mix of a few of these realms and possibly other realms I have not mentioned in this book such as "The Knights Paladin" and "Mystic Angels", as described in Doreen Virtue's **Earth Angels** and **Realms of the Earth Angels** books.

- Higher Self (The part of you that has all the human lives – Your Eternal Self – your light body the color of your soul – Access your Akashic Records here).

- God, Goddess, Source (Gold Sunlight).

- Arch angels (Light Beings – not human bodies, different colors, work with and around helping people they aren't working in other dimensions, specifically working with humankind on Earth, they have a very brilliant light energy).

- Ascended Masters, Avatars, and Saints (have walked the Earth previously in human form, their understanding and energy is a little denser).

- Guides and Guardian Angels (your personal guides and angels can come and go as you are working on certain things and old friends from many lifetimes ago).

- Elementals (nature spirits, crystals, leprechauns, fairies, elves, animal kingdom, mermaids, water sprites, plant spirits, tree spirits).

- Deceased People (are loved ones who have passed over and are with you working as guides).

- Human.

GUIDES

"If you could see the loving beings and Guides that walk with you throughout your life, you would never again live in fear."

~ Sibyl Harmony

You Have Personal Guides

Everyone has loving beings around them. You will often hear them called Guides. Your guides love you unconditionally. Your guides are here to assist you. Your guides are here to protect you in your mission and purpose here on earth and to help you evolve.

Usually everyone has at least two primary guides watching over them. Depending on the realm you are closest to or as you develop your awareness different guides will show up and start working with you as is appropriate in different times of your spiritual development. Such as ascended Masters, or arch angels, star beings, mermaids, etc. Your higher self and at least one deceased loved one or more from your family around you.

One thing to know is that there is a hierarchy of guides, and at the higher levels, these guides generally can't help you unless you ask, the exception to this rule is if you are in a life-threatening situation, they may intervene on your behalf if they are protecting you being able to fulfill your mission. This is a part of the Divine Laws and an agreement that they make as guides.

Who are your guides? Well, usually they are like old friends that your soul has known for your whole life (such as Grandparents you were close to) or throughout many lifetimes, (such as guardian angels, Masters, and elementals) and they love you unconditionally.

You may also have guides that come in or show up to help you at certain times or with important projects in your life (such as writing a book, having a baby, starting a business, making art, healers such as; nurse, doctor, shaman, energetic healer, massage therapist, animal healers, rescue workers or soldiers going off to war, social activists, environmental activists, teachers, scientists and innovators who develop new technology, community organizers, spiritual teachers, home makers, etc.) there are specific guides and masters for each of these areas.

Guides can be especially helpful to us in life if we want to create, manifest, evolve, and grow spiritually. We can connect with those that have gone before us or the ancient beings trained in the old ways on this planet, animal spirits, and those from other dimensions.

Imagine you are going on a trip, you might want to decide on the destination, book your plane tickets and hotel, but you will certainly need someone who can fly the plane and knows how to get you to your intended destination safely.

Similarly, when entering spiritual realms, it's a good idea to contact your guides so they have permission to assist you to move through the inner worlds more easily.

We learned about the chakras of our higher self and now will learn how to develop a better relationship with our higher self as our Guide.

Who is the Higher Self?

The highest realm is the realm of the higher self. I consider the Holy Ghost our higher self. It is the third aspect of "Father, Son, and Holy Ghost" or "Source, God/Goddess, Higher Self" that completes the Holy Trinity. Your higher self is the Master Teacher of all things to you to bring us into alignment.

Another way to understand your higher self is - it is you come back from the future where you have already evolved and learned lessons that can assist and teach you what you need to know in this present moment. Soul exists in all timelines at once, past, present, and future. This is how it is possible for your future or past higher self to communicate and teach you knowledge and wisdom in your current life.

As we develop, we begin to understand that WE ARE the avatars, Earth angels, ascended Masters, and Goddesses. We are choosing to evolve here in "Earth School". As we continue to awaken, this can be called an ascension process and as we grow there is a choice as to whether we continue to incarnate assisting Earth and humankind or choose a more galactic purpose in other parts of the universe or other dimensions.

Higher Self vs. Personality

You may think you are your personality. Such as if your name is Ann, the second child and own a house on Broadway and work as an Executive Assistant to the VP of Legal Ease Law Firm. Your higher self is not Ann the personality who does and has all those things, your higher self is the part of you that has had many past lifetimes, many names and personalities, and has access to all of the knowledge from those incarnations within your soul.

The higher self exists in the higher realms and is connected to you and your physical body (personality) through the higher chakras.

Using the techniques I teach, in healing, recognizing, and clearing the unconscious energy that is not yours, allows you to receive downloads from your higher self's knowledge and wisdom into your physical body and energy field. This is the definition of awakening your consciousness, it facilitates the healing of your mind, body, spirit, and environment. Balance and harmony are the spiritual spoils of doing your energy work. In truth, if we all opened our hearts to our higher self and used our spiritual power, the oceans would purify as we'd make better decisions about pollution and respect, making a better world for us, our families, our children, and all of life.

Violet Light, My Higher Self

When I first started doing this work, I met my higher self. She appeared to me as a violet light. I noticed she was always around. Guiding me through my day. Flashing her light during sessions and healings confirming what I was seeing and feeling in my readings. She would even tuck me in at night and say "Goodnight." Finally, I asked her,

"Who are you?". She said, "I'm you." I said, "No, I'm me. Who are YOU?" She didn't back down from her answer that "she was me." So, I let it go, and then she was shown to me as a woman from one of my past incarnations, she was still illuminated by the violet light, when I looked into her eyes (the windows of the soul and how to recognize Spirit Connections) I saw the truth, "yes, you are me," my higher self. So, now I know when seeing the violet light, throughout my day and in anything I do, she is always there for me, my personality Sibyl doesn't question her anymore. My best friend, Higher Self.

Exercise for Connecting with your Higher Self, as a Guide

Everyone can talk to their soul or higher self. Just sit in a quiet place with pen and a piece of paper. Give yourself 10-20 minutes. Turn phone off or silence your notifications, or put a timer on, let the children know you'll be offline for 10-20 minutes or as long as their cartoon show takes to finish.

You can choose, just for this exercise, to allow yourself to let go of any feeling thoughts or issues from your day, taking some deep relaxing breaths, and breathing in the feeling of peace, and breathing out any stress, frustrations, and issues that are affecting you today, just feeling your body agree to relax for now. In this moment. Your breath opens you up to the higher realms and helps you connect with spirit and your psychic abilities.

Closing your eyes, take a moment to notice how your body feels, and ask your higher self "what does my body need right now?" and let the higher self communicate with you through your body and notice any thoughts, feelings, images, or sounds, or words. Acknowledge anything you get, without judgment, it doesn't have to make sense immediately, just allow your hand to connect to the stream of wisdom coming through from your higher self and write it down, draw, or scribble. Ask again, "show me anything in my mind and body that I need to know" then just write whatever comes through.

Know this is your creative imagination at work, there is NO WRONG WAY. You are allowing your playful imagination, your pure energy to connect and give you guidance from an unhindered state.

You'll always get the message you need. That is the message that is meant for you right now.

James's story

James did this exercise. When I asked him how it went, he told me he didn't really get anything just heard the words "we love you". He said it seemed like they were his soul, or higher self group and they just kept saying, "we love you".

James was frustrated that this was the only message coming through and they didn't say something else.

I explained to him, "haven't you been wanting a new relationship?" He said, "yes". I said, "Well the foundation of any relationship is about loving ourself first." That was EXACTLY what he needed to hear. "We love you".

Many times, we (our ego) expect spirit to communicate in full sentences and complicated mental responses. However, spirit is pure, not interested in our "ego". Some of the most profound lessons are when we allow ourselves to actually "hear" the guidance being given.

It can oftentimes be simple. And until you accept the message and reflect upon what that simple message means for you, spirit will be relentless in making sure you receive your soul's message.

If you didn't hear anything, or if you doubted what you received, just be your own private investigator and record the sounds, words, thoughts, feelings, and things that are happening in your life or around you in a notebook or journal as you practice. Speaking to spirit requires an openness - an allowing, without us trying to "control" what we think we "should" be getting. Your guides will show up, your higher self will ALWAYS answer you. It IS YOU, the most pure and knowing YOU, but you might not be aware of the answers until the timing is right for you to receive them. Keep up the practice, keep asking and listening the messages will come!

Remembering Childhood Guides

Many people may have communicated with spirit guides and elemental guides since childhood, and their experience may have been brushed aside as "imaginary friends" or "just your imagination" or told "they aren't real". When in actuality they could have been your angels, fairies, or other guides!

When parents ask their children questions, they forget that they might be getting answers from a wise old soul, in a young human body. Because children have just come from a place of unconditional love, spirit, and wisdom – the God worlds, Source Creation, their hearts are open and are full of light. They can see, sense, and understand spirit communication in the simple beautiful way that only a child can unless we as adults reconnect to our own childlike innocence.

So, remember when speaking with your children or wise ones in young bodies, to really listen and validate their higher self, intuition, and wisdom that they are bringing in. Try to stay in a place of curiosity about what they are feeling or seeing and let them talk to you or show you and explain to you that wisdom they are still so close to. Record or write down what they tell you or tell them to draw it so they can keep that channel of light open and always know who they are as soul, as they mature in the human consciousness. Sometimes, children see monsters or things they are afraid of, so we can help them bring in their light and energy for protection and teach them how to invite in their protective angels and guides to help them know they aren't alone or in danger. In my advanced book, we'll talk about how to help psychic medium children develop, understand, and control their gifts.

Come as Children to the Sacred ~ A story about the first channeled message I remember receiving from my guides.

As a child around age six, I was very used to laughing, singing, and playing with the elemental spirits around my home and in nature. Fairies, elves, leprechauns, dancing flowers, and tree spirits would make themselves known to me as I played and enjoyed their company and silliness.

One beautiful warm day, I was playing outside on our lawn. The sun was high and shining down on my shoulders when all of a sudden, I heard a kind and comforting male voice speak into my mind "*You are not alone*". Used to hearing nature spirits as I was, I didn't think too much about it, and quickly returned to playing and said to myself innocently "okay... *I'm not alone*" and continued playing. But this voice had a different quality to it, a very ancient warm quality, his voice wasn't at all silly and left a sense of what it feels like to be safe around a trusted adult, the voice left a solid loving imprint upon my memory, something that in later life would be very important for me.

Later, I thought perhaps this voice was a guide, or divine spirit, and I was curious to see if I could learn who it was that left such a wonderful message for me, so I decided to ask consciously who It/He – was. Here's what came through.

Channeled Transmission with Spirit as adult in meditation.

Who are you?" I said.

Beginning of transmission…

"I am the God of your childhood. I am the one that said *you are not alone*. I am the Sun millions of years old. I have watched over you. Never controlled you. I have loved you and been with you always. I have loved you enough to let you learn your lessons. I have witnessed and celebrated your joy. I have stood beside you in your pain. Not fixing you so that you could grow as a soul. I was with you oh mermaid when you sang with the dolphins. Summer your name was and "Ah" the little-known Sumerian Goddess of Dawn. You spoke Gods ancient words for thousands of years as Sybil Oracle. I was there when you were a retarded boy so that you could learn innocence and compassion. We rode oh Templar Knight of Good Service and did faithful deeds. We shared the ancient secrets of healing. You walked thought the valley of death. So brave to come here again to this wonderful, beautiful sometimes dark shadow place called earth."

End of transmission

I am sharing this story so that you know you are never too young, or too old, you are just as special as me and can receive all manner of guidance. It is your birthright to be connected and receive messages from spirit.

What is most important is to simply ask questions from a curious heart, and know that sprit will always answer you, and when you are most open and receptive and have released our own "expectation" of "how" spirit is going to communicate, you will receive your divine answers in divine time.

Empower Yourself with Guides

We are each students, here on Earth. We learn from our parents, school teachers, friends that we admire and trust, and our experience. Here, I would like to include that we also learn from our guides and spiritual teachers and inner Masters. This relationship can be one of the most important and empowering relationships of your life. I'm not the last word on guides, and you might meet or work with guides I've never worked with. There are an unlimited number of Masters, Goddesses, and star beings, and elementals that you are meant to learn with and from, and also guides from your past lives and your higher self. Your guides are always with you. Your job is to trust what you receive from a place of love, wisdom, validation, things you haven't thought of, opening you up to new possibilities that are greater than you would have ever imagined.

Learning to Trust Yourself

For years I studied with a healer. He was a great teacher, and I learned a lot from him (including discernment). He had a guide he was working but he didn't like to speak about who his guide was. One day I overheard him talking to his guide and asked him about it. He said "he" had a great guide, and that "my guides were false". I was shocked that this close teacher of mine would invalidate *My Guides.* He also said I could only have one! I immediately knew that was not true for me.

It became clear that I had mastered my inner knowingness enough to discern what was true for me. In that moment – the student became the master of this lesson.

NOT MY GUIDE!

When I was training and working with a shaman, she instructed me to chant the name of a God like being in meditation. Although I felt no connection to that particular guide, I did as I was instructed by my teacher. I chanted the name in mediation every day. Toward the last day of the third week, I heard a loud stern voice say, "WHAT DO YOU WANT?!".

"Wow, sorry," I said. I believe the guide also knew that we had no work, and no agreement with each other in this time, confirming what my intuition already knew. So, I stopped chanting to him after that experience.

Developing trust in your own feelings and connection with certain guides is paramount to having a fruitful and productive relationship with the guides who are here to work with you.

David's story

David was a student of mine and he wanted to be able to communicate with his guides as he felt like connecting would be supportive to him and guide him on his path and life's mission.

So, I tuned into David's energy field and saw a connection to Jesus. I told him, "I see you have a strong connection to Jesus." He said, "No. That's not going to work, I'm not religious" and then revealed in the same conversation that he had already had Jesus come to him on a walk through the woods. But he "avoided talking to him and kept walking". As we said before – you cannot force anyone to connect. In this world, the spiritual laws dictate that you have "Free Will". You make these agreements to work with certain guides in other lifetimes on the other side. So, David exercised his free will for several more years, still hoping to connect with a guide. One day David came to the realization that Jesus "wasn't religious" but instead is a powerful force of love and healing on this planet.

David started walking in the woods every day and developed a relationship with Jesus. He realized he had had many lifetimes working with this powerful guide. He is doing very well and works as a healer manifesting a life he loves.

Spirit Guides

Arch Angels: Arch angels are high vibrational, non-denominational beings of light who have never been human and have agreed to serve in the God Worlds to help humankind for those who ask. They are usually androgynous and can come across as either masculine or feminine energy. They can see past what we think of as "flaws" and only see who we really are as another "worthy child of God and Spark of Creator".

Arch angels have been around since always, and they are even recorded in times of Atlantis and Ancient Egypt. There are hieroglyphs in the ancient pyramids that read sacred incantations "If you can summon this Arch Angel your life will profoundly change."

No task is too big or too small to call upon your arch angel team. They are available instantly and can be in several locations at one time so never worry that you are taking an angel from someone else.

Arch Angel Michael

His name means "he who is like God" and is the protector of humans. His color appears to us as a bright cobalt blue so bright and vivid it can look purple. He has a light sword ready to cut away any lower energies and is the Patron Saint of Rescue Workers and Guardians. Police, firemen, military, and everyday selfless heroes. He clears away fear, can help to repair broken things, assist with technology, and can help when conducting a space clearing for home and business, and creating safe space. He is also the angel that can help you open the doors to your life's purpose.

When driving in a dark area one night I was feeling a little lost and I called on him. Instantly a purple light appeared in front of my car and lead me home. Even if you don't see him when you ask, know he will be there in a few seconds.

Don't hesitate to call upon Archangel Michael to "escort" lower beings out of your space or energy field. Consider him your "Angelic Bouncer."

Arch Angel Rafael

Arch angel Rafael is a healing angel. His name means "friend of God". Rafael's energy feels gentle and strong like a friend and may feel like a gentle pulsing when his presence is near. His color is green and yellow or gold. He works with all kinds of healing.

He heals pets and children. He also helps to heal addictions. When you call this friendly arch angel, he will be there in seconds to help anyone.

When I first started doing healing on others, I would call in Archangel Raphael to help me. I was new and questioning whether he was actually helping me (I'm strongly clairvoyant and I am a "seeing is believing" personality), so I asked him to "show me if any of this was real or if I was just imagining it" after I asked, he literally popped out of my hands and manifested in front of me energetically! I was totally shocked! I thanked him as this made it real to me. I was in fact working with the angels.

Arch Angel Metatron

Metatron is one of the arch angels that was one of only two arch angels that were in human bodies before. He was a Prophet Enoch and worked directly alongside God, Creator in an angelic form.

Metatron's energy may show up as a watermelon color or violet. He is great working with young people, organizing priorities, helping you get motivated and grounding your energy. He helps heal mental issues such as depression, ADHD (Attention Dialed into Higher Dimensions) and his specialty is healing with Sacred Geometry.

Arch Angel Gabriel

Arch angel Gabriel may appear to you as bright yellow, orange, or gold and, more than the other arch angels, may come across as either strongly masculine or feminine depending on what you are asking for help with. Gabriel is present for childbirth, writing, and artistic endeavors and helped me in the writing of this book.

Gabriel is non-denominational like all arch angels, and you can call upon him/her for fertility, safe childbirth, and caring for very young children.

Arch Angel Ariel

Arch angel Arial helped King Solomon capture demons and put them to work building his temple. She appears as a medium pink color and shows herself often with a lion's head. She is brave and helps with wild animals, particularly large cats, and winged creatures. I call upon her to help with animals in distress.

Ascended Masters

Ascended Masters have walked planet Earth in human bodies, and have either come back (reincarnated), or stayed here to help humankind.

They have had many lifetimes and their presence spans every land mass on the planet from Africa, Australia, Asia, Europe, North and South America and are oftentimes considered or called "The Wise One's", "Spiritual Masters", "Old Soul's". Many times, they can be spiritual leaders or the faces of religion and different spiritual paths.

Jesus Christ, Yeshua, or an earlier incarnation of the same soul named Melchizedek produced mel-kee-zah-deck (a powerful shaman priest) you may also hear of his energy referred to as "Christ Consciousness" or Cristos.

His energy usually appears as a bright blue color with a yellow or gold aura, and you might smell Frankincense and Myrrh if he is in your presence.

He teaches about love and forgiveness and is amazing at manifestation. He will protect anyone that asks. He loves us unconditionally. When working with Jesus you may be offered a spiritual vision of a "chalice" as a symbol of initiation.

He is from the planet Arcturus and is closely connected to horses. Who are also highly evolved spirit beings that hail from Arcturus.

Mother Mary

Mother Mary understands all kinds of healing. She is often referred to as "mother" as she cares for children, women, and is everyone's Mother.

Her energy may come across as the color corn blue. She will teach you and help you to become a better mother and to respect "mothers and motherhood".

When I became a mother, I didn't have any idea how to do it. Mothers weren't seen as important or as valuable as fathers or men in general so my own understanding of what it meant to be a mother wasn't fully developed. She knows that being a mother is important work and one of the most difficult and rewarding tasks of our lives.

You might be surprised to know that she can help us learn what it is to run a home, work, pay bills, and taxes.

In her own time and experience she had to learn and do all these tasks within the context of a hostile Roman empire.

She will be your Mother and show you how you can nurture and re-parent your inner child. She is queen of the angels, a teacher of magic, healing, reincarnation, the cycles of life, death, and rebirth, and has influence over bodies of water.

A simple prayer or blessing you can do is to ask for Mother Mary to bless your water every time you and your family drink it.

Mary Magdalene pronounced MAG-duh-leen

Her name means *Mary the Magnificent*. She studied in the Temple of Isis, and was the teacher of Jesus, some believe she was also his wife. Her method of healing was through human touch and connection. Oftentimes, when she conducted a healing, she would get into bed with people and hug them (men and women). I see her energy as a beautiful bright magenta color.

The "church" was not prepared to accept a powerful female as a teacher or in the power of loving people back to health, so they dis-empowered her and minimalized her gifts by calling her a prostitute.

Call upon Mary Magdalene to help you with healings of all kinds, physical, women's issues, and relationships. She is also a powerful healer associated with bodies of water.

Vishnu

Vishnu is one of the Hindu Gods that works beside Brahma and Shiva to persevere the world. Call upon him for harmony, protection, mercy, and feeling good about the future. He is a benevolent loving deity that incarnated in animal form before becoming human.

Ganesh

Ganesh is the Hindu God who has the head of an elephant and a human body. Call upon him to overcome obstacles and create abundance. He is very supportive of anyone who is in a bind and can help you clear your path, and get things started. I see him as a gold color.

White Buffalo Calf Woman

White Buffalo Calf Woman is a prophetess. She appeared to the Lakota Native Americans and is here to amplify prayers and bridge the connection to heaven and earth. When you see white animals call upon her to bring world peace and help with the environment. I see her energy as a pearl white.

Quan Yin

Quan Yin is the Buddha of compassion and forgiveness. She has earned Buddhahood and chooses to stay here on a mission until all human beings are enlightened. Her energy is comparable to that of Mother Mary. She may come across as red, peach, and light pink.

If you call on her, she will help you, however she will ask you to reciprocate by helping others when you are healed.

She oftentimes appears and works with powerful protection dragons. You can call on these benevolent protective dragons and Quan Yin for healing, magic, and protection.

Ishtar

Ishtar is the Sumerian and Babylonian Goddess of Peace and War, married to the Sumerian God of Harvest, also known in her earlier incarnation as Inanna, First Woman. Her brother was Utt, a powerful male god working with her. Her star lineage is from the Orion Star System. I see her as violet and pearl white.

Ishtar is the founder of the Sisterhood of Ishtar which is a group of beings who are here to help empower womankind, and while those in this sisterhood are not trained to do healings, they are taught to do readings and teach humans about "consciousness". The sisterhood helps women learn boundaries and strength for the good of all and is connected to large cats. I am one in the Sisterhood of Ishtar, and in a past life I was a lesser Goddess of dawn.

Every woman is made in the image of the Goddess.

Isis

Isis is an Egyptian Goddess. Her energy comes across as a light pink color. She works to heal women's issue, relationships, marriage, healing, magic, mothering. She was a devoted wife and mother and healed her husband.

She symbolizes strength and female power and is connected with Temple Cats and will help you make time for the things in life you love.

Isis trained Mary Magdalene and Mother Mary in the Temple of Isis. She will appear when there is really big, important healing work.

She is one of the most powerful healing guides, her star lineage is from the Sirius.

Merlin

Merlin was a powerful wizard, the quintessential Magician who is connected to King Arthurs's court and Camelot and helped train spiritual teachers and healers learn to focus their energies and abilities. He may come across as many colors, but to me I sense him as green and blue.

Saint Francis

Saint Francis of Assisi was born to a wealthy Italian cloth merchant and renounced his inheritance to follow an ascetic spiritual path.

He volunteered at hospitals and attended to the sick. He gained many followers and became known for his ability to communicate with animals, and healing "sick" environments. You can call on him when family does not understand your choices, and to help with animals and animal communication. I sense his energy as a silver/blue.

The prayer for Saint Francis is in the back of the book in the Prayers Index.

Saint Germaine

Saint Germaine comes across with violet stars and sparkling lights – basically a star shower whenever he's around. He is connected to the seven violet flames. He and his twin soul Porchsa help light workers toward their mission of realizing world peace.

Saint Germaine was loved by the working class and royalty alike. He was always invited to attend social events where royalty were present. In 1700 France, Saint Germaine was renowned for his musical, and magical abilities. Many people say he had a "fountain of youth elixir" as it was often said that he had been seen over spans of hundreds of years and looked as if he hadn't aged a single day.

Animal Totems

Animal Totems are animal guides that are here on Earth and help to bring specific medicine to heal and guide you throughout your life. Usually, you will have one or two primary animal spirit totems that stay with you always and others that come and go that are here teach you their different medicine for a specific reason or at a time when it is needed in your life.

One of my animal spirit totems in this life is Wolf. In past lives I lived and worked closely with wolves and they are now my spiritual protectors and helpers. The medicine they bring and that I am learning from them is service and loyalty.

Raven is another of my animal spirit totems. They can move through this dimension and cross over to the other side. As a medium they help me connect to the magic and medicine of the other side during my healings and readings.

Elemental Guides

Elemental guides are those who live on Earth but in a different dimension and are connected to nature and the environment. Of these you might be familiar with are fairies (flower, plant, water, wood, fire, metal, earth, air), elves, leprechauns, mermaids, dragons, unicorns, Pegasus, crystals, and tree spirits.

If you want to connect to elementals in this dimension, then the most important thing is you have to believe. When you don't believe in them it hurts them and they go away. I say I DO BELIEVE! I DO BELIEVE IN FAIRIES! They also like silly energy, music, parties, fun and dancing.

Although leprechauns never give their names until they can trust that you won't tell anyone. They believe if you have their name you can get their JUJU. So, you might get a code name at first *wink wink*.

To connect with mermaids, I go to the ocean or water spirits are around lakes or other bodies of water. As a general rule, the more water around the easier it is to receive any spiritual information. Because you're dealing with energy and water conducts energy. Water helps any guide to come in more clearly.

To connect with star or celestial beings it can be helpful to go outside at night and speak to the heavens, stars, and galaxies.

For tree spirits go and hug a tree. It's great practice to talk to trees and receive healing from them. Just pick a tree. Sit with it. If you touch the tree you will start to feel a pulsing energy. You can ask the tree questions. Notice your thoughts and feelings as this is your clairs working to communicate with them. Seeing tree spirits is a sign that your consciousness is awakening to the other dimensions. Plus, you can receive amazing healing letting them send you healing energy and gently reset your biorhythms by hugging them and asking for a healing.

There are quite literally galaxies of guides you can work with and call upon. For me, I truly believe you get a different kind of support from different guides from different realms.

Visualization for connecting with your guides

Relax in a comfortable place that is quiet and you won't be disturbed. Closing your eyes brings you into a bigger world, the world of spirit and energy. Ask Creator, Source to reveal who your guides are, maybe what their names are, what their specialty is, or what their medicine is, and how they are here to help you, if you've known them before and where they know you from? These are all questions that you can ask out loud gently and with a light heart.

Playfulness and allowing your imagination to flow is allowed and helpful. Allow yourself to breathe deeply in through your nose, and out as you like.

Notice if you are relaxed and feeling safe. Allow any situations, issues, feelings, and thoughts of the day to be released for now through your breath, you can also ask any heavy energy to wait outside until you're done with your visualization.

Allow your face to soften, your jaw to relax. Allow your digestive organs and belly to relax ... as you continue breathing, let your arms release like ropes unwinding and releasing tension ... release the muscles and tendons in your legs so they are relaxed and connected to the floor, the earth, or your seat.

Imagine that you are in a beautiful garden, with trees blowing in a gentle breeze. See the beautiful flowers and take in their scent. A small bird is singing a song. A clear babbling brook flows in the background.

You have a sense and a knowing that a loving presence is surrounding you.

As you sense this presence your attention beckons you to an ornate archway illuminated with golden sunlight that takes you to higher realms. As you move toward the arch way ... you notice ascending steps, you can feel yourself relax even further as you are lovingly guided and begin to effortlessly float up to the place where your guides are. A life affirming mist envelops you ... as you breathe it in you feel amazingly safe and clear, and you continue to float upward. Your awareness stops floating as you reach the realm where you will meet your guide today.

When you stop floating you look around and see a translucent veil and you know instinctively you are safe to move through it. On the other side of the veil, you feel the same loving presence that you felt below and now you look down and notice the feet of your guide. Notice if they have shoes, or sandals, are barefoot, or are not human feet. Notice how their presence feels, their energy, notice any sounds, smells, thoughts, surroundings, environment, or lights. Notice if you have known them before.

As you take this in, they invite you to sit with them. You can ask them any questions you may have … you may receive answers in visions, words, feelings, or thoughts.

Even if you don't see them know they are here.

You can ask them, have I known you before this lifetime.

You can ask them what they are here to help you learn or do.

You can ask them for a name.

You can ask for any specific guidance as well.

Listen, feel, and be. Know that you are bringing back the love, messages, and connection whether it is conscious or unconscious.

Take a moment to thank your guide and feel your awareness come back down to earth, through the veil, down the stairs, through the archway, back into the garden and into the present moment. You are grounded and bringing the love, light, feeling, energy, and new connection with your guides.

If you don't receive an answer now, know that they have received your questions and you will receive them when the time is right. Just trust and relax that you have made this connection with your guide and with this sacred realm. Universe, Source, Creator knows that you are reaching out to connect.

Wiggle your toes, and fingers, take several deep breaths, move your face, and blink your eyes. Come back into your present senses.

In the weeks and time after this visualization be aware of any signs and guidance, feelings, dreams, sensations, smells that you might be receiving. Pay attention to any names you hear or that someone may give you out of the blue, notice the timing of any synchronistic events and pay attention to "ah ha" moments.

OUR INNER CHILD

One Christmas holiday season, when my granddaughter was four years old. I decided to have a fun project and put a gingerbread house together with her.

I let her explore her own creativity and was truly present with her. I let her be creative and we had great fun making a big mess. I saw that she was eating some of the candy decorations when I wasn't looking. I didn't say anything about that. We laughed and played. Maggie made giant blobs of icing on the walls of the gingerbread house then stuck piles of candy on top. Instead of trying to make it look perfect. I decided it was the memory of us having fun and validating her creativity that was more important that day. When we bring our presence, we are sitting in sacred energy with someone. It is prayer in action or being.

At one point she stopped and looked deeply into my eyes. It was a beautiful moment for both of us. It was as if her soul was connecting with mine. I looked back at her and said in my heart: I see you, I am here with you. We spoke no words, but it was a gift we gave to each other that will last forever.

The eyes are the windows of the soul. We are deep and ancient beings. All of us are.

Later that night my grandson Dylan, 10, had a nightmare. He was yelling out in his sleep for help. He woke up crying. I went to him and held him as he wept, missing his mother, who had not been in his life for two years. He was so sad. I just held him as he cried. I was grateful I could be there for him.

What if there is no one there? What if we are alone in the night fearful and lonely? Even as adults we all carry the pain of separation, illness, death, and loss. Many nights, I woke up crying and there was no one there. As this is true for all of us. What if our inner child just wanted to be held and loved?

What do we do when there is no Grandma coming to comfort us in the dark night? How do we heal ourselves when we didn't get what we needed as children? How do we get what we need if a parent passes on? Or if we weren't validated and loved for who we were?

How do we heal the wounds of feeling abandoned, controlled, abused, helpless, or heartbroken?

The process begins with our heart. It is in the center of our chest and some call it the heart chakra. The first step is to sit with our feelings and truly feel them. Most people tend to stuff down those feelings. Do the opposite and allow yourself to feel them.

I acknowledge that when you go inside you will find pain, fear, walls, and resentments. However, that pain is a treasure that is your sacred witness.

For the next step, open your heart and ask for grace. You can look to the sacred divine mother, mother earth, your loving guides, the angels, or the Christ energy for comfort. Feel the grace. In your heart you will find the beautiful presence of your soul. Your whole life will change from feelings of loneliness, sadness, or resentment to one where someone is there for you.

For so many, this is a dream come true. You will have what everyone is searching to find. The love, the peace and the presence that are all inside of you.

This is how we heal the inner child.

Exercise to Heal Your Inner Child

We have all been hurt. When we are hurt, a part of us splinters off, closes down, or disconnects from our true self.

If our parents weren't able to help us feel safe, loved, protected, and valued, we are responsible for re-parenting our own inner child.

Sending the love and healing that is needed to our inner child hearts, minds, and bodies can bring transformation, healing, and alignment into our adult lives so that we can live a healthier existence. It is never too late to create a happy childhood!

One way I like to approach this healing is to call in soft, loving energy, like Mother Mary, Quan Yin, Mary Magdala, or Isis. You can also call in your mother, and your higher self, or call in a loving safe father healing, through the sun, Christ energy, your father, or a loving guide.

Sitting or lying down, imagine healing light pour into your heart, feel the presence of the unconditional love of mother or father.

Imagine your inner child drawing you back to a house, an age, or a situation where they need your help. Trust your inner child will show you the right time and place.

Take in the house or scene where you find yourself and sense how your inner child felt being there. Go in and find your inner child. Notice if they will talk to you. See if they will trust you. Soften your face and tell them, "I'm you from the future come back to help you, if that's ok." Tell them they can have all the time they need, and you can always be here when they need you.

If your inner child is tired, scared, angry, or throwing a temper tantrum, just check in with them, feel what they are upset about? See what it is that they need? It is your job to heal and re-parent your inner child. You get to give them the love and attention you wanted as a child. You get to tend the garden of their needs.

You can tell them "I'm sorry what happened to you". And just listen to them and feel what they need you to know, hear, or feel. You can tell them "I love you and I won't leave you".

Be kind, gentle, and patient with your inner child, it's okay to just wait and be there.

Your inner child might need to play or have fun. You can ask them to show you what they most love to do, ask if they want to plan fun stuff with other children, you can ask if they'd like to come with you and experience another time and place together? Whatever is happening, just love, listen, and play with your inner child.

When you are ready to end the exercise, you can invite them into your heart. You care about how they feel. And look forward to cuddling, caring, protecting, and having fun with them. Your innocence and joy being fully restored to all the places in your heart.

Hands on Healing Exercise

To do hands on healing simply call your guides or higher self into your hands. I use a method I call "Unbending Intention". This is where you are crystal clear on your intention to heal and are NOT wishy washy in your thoughts or energy. You are simply declaring "this _____ is healing NOW!"

Ground yourself using the grounding breath exercise from above and feel free to start with a prayer.

Start the exercise: Start by calling your guides into your hands (I usually have my palms open to the heavens, you can rub your hands together or use your breath), feel the energy in your hands and notice if they activated, pulsing, warm, tingling, cooling, use your clair senses to sense the energy from your guides or your higher self coming into your hands. This energy comes from above you. Let it flow down through your hands.

You are sending loving energy to your guides and self and receiving the healing frequencies needed from them. They know what to do and what your body needs. Your guides will escort your hands to where they belong.

First, bring your attention to feel, know, and sense the skin, then sense to the muscles, bones, nervous system, and organs. Let the guides move your energy. Life is movement, so feel into if there is any blocked, frayed, or heavy energy, you can keep your hands here for several minutes or until your guides or hands escort you to another section of your body.

When you are complete, you might get a signal, for me my guides flash a light, you might feel release, or lightness, you can also muscle test or use your pendulum to check in and confirm for yourself, if the healing is complete.

When you are done clap your hands three times, which clears the energy, release the guides from your hands and say, "Thank you, this healing is complete!" You may also wash your hands afterwards as well, to clear the energy from your healing tools (hands ☺). This is you giving the healing boundaries so that the energy cycle is complete for this particular healing.

DIVINATION

Divination is the ability to receive guidance and information from your higher self, signs, symbols, tools, or guides. We can do this for ourselves, loved ones, or clients.

Many say this is a highly evolved ability and you're either born with it or it takes time to develop it. But you may already be doing it naturally. And just not realize how.

I work with all kinds of divination tools in my healing and teaching practice such as Tarot & Oracle cards, pendulums, symbolic healing, crystals, oils, and candle divination. I go into depth in my Advanced Book and Training Courses for those who want to learn how to heal others and have a healing practice with clients.

In this next section, I will show you how to work with a pendulum using a system called "dowsing". We will use this to diagnose and heal a chakra. This a great place to start so you develop trust in your intuitive relationship with your tools in order to heal yourself.

Working with a Pendulum

A pendulum is a divination tool that can be made of a natural stone like crystal, a piece of wood, or a metal ore (the crystal will have spirit energy within it) that is suspended from a string, or chain, that allows the weighted point to swing freely back and forth.

Pendulums are great tools as they respond to the electric magnetic field and various energetic pulses to help humans connect with unseen natural and energetic forces.

As a spiritual tool, pendulums can be programmed to give you clear answers yes and no as well as to heal and balance the energetic body. The latter is what we will be doing here.

Develop a Relationship with your Pendulum

Using any divination tool requires a conscious grounding and connection before you get started working with it. This ensures you understand how it will communicate with you so you can trust the answers you are receiving. I like to run my energy to make sure I am grounded. I then like to call my guides (I call in Arch Angel Michael and the spirit that resides in the crystal of the pendulum I am working with (some people call this spirit a Deva – or a nature spirit). I like to hold it and speak to it, so it gets used to my energy.

Basic Calibration

Hold the pendulum three to six inches away from your body in front of your heart and place your other hand that's not holding the pendulum underneath the point of the pendulum about three inches away. This creates an energetic field for your pendulum to communicate with you in.

Invite your pendulum to show you a "yes", allow your pendulum to start swinging or moving and observe its movements. It may swing backwards and forwards or horizontally left to right or in a circle (clockwise or counterclockwise). Pay attention to this movement and say, "thank you".

Now ask for your pendulum to show you its "no". Give it a moment to change direction and observe again how it is communicating. Make sure you are breathing and not holding your breath so that your life force is circulating.

Now, you can receive your "yes and no" answers. If you aren't getting any movement, you may need to clear it of any stagnant energy. You can run it under water, you can use sage, incense or palo santo, or you can put in the sunlight for four-hours or use the moon cycles to charge and clear it (for instance: place your pendulum out under the moon, the night before the full moon you get the maximum "waxing energy" growth supercharge. If you leave out through the full moon it clears the energy of your pendulum and brings a balanced charge as it is at its full energy. Place your pendulum out the night before the "dark moon" for maximum "waning energy" and the new moon cycle will clear your pendulum and charge it with new beginnings energy).

Then test again for your yes and no.

I like to start a chakra balance with the heart chakra. I believe the heart chakra is the most important chakra to heal first as it can be the one that is most easily closed down or blocked, which in turn blocks our ability to heal ourselves. It is only when your heart is open that your abilities truly open up and blossom, and your life path can open. Keep in mind that your heart will only open as much as is appropriate for you in each moment. That is why regularly checking and balancing of the heart chakra is an excellent practice.

Most humans are vibrating in their lower or higher chakras, you might be able to recognize this, as the lower chakras are where "physical survival" resides, and emotions and control issues can be a main theme. Especially during hard times, the lower chakras can be overactive or out of balance.

If someone is mostly vibrating in the higher chakras, they can be over analytical, "heady", spiritually minded but perhaps un-grounded.

Starting with the heart chakra place the pendulum six to eight inches away from the body directly in front of the heart chakra area (in the middle of your chest). Holding your hand still with the pendulum make sure you have three to six inches of cord or chain and allow the pendulum to tune into your energy for a moment. The pendulum will start to move or swing on its own.

Note the different movements your pendulum may make:

Clockwise - If the pendulum starts to move in a clockwise motion when in front of the chakra that indicates it is open and in balance.

Counterclockwise - If the pendulum starts to move counterclockwise direction, that indicates that your chakra is out of balance.

Side to Side or Shimmy - If the pendulum moves side to side or shimmy or wobbly, this indicates that the chakra is trying to balance but is stuck.

No movement at all – If the pendulum does not move when initially placed in front of the chakra, the energy center is blocked.

Healing or Balancing Your Chakra

First pick the chakra you want to work on and find a quiet place to do your healing.

Now watch the video on how to run your energy and ground and run your energy for a few minutes.

Click the link below to watch the Running Your Energy video first the follow along and watch the Healing and Balancing your Chakras video for practice!

https://sibylharmony.com/white-rainbow-videos

Call in your healing guides.

Imagine the chakra you are working with in front of you using the image of a chakra to guide you on what you might seeing or feeling. What we are looking for in this exercise is any pictures, devices, implements, lower energies, cords, cracks or breaks or misalignment.

Front View of Chakra
showing the Moment of Now with clear energy

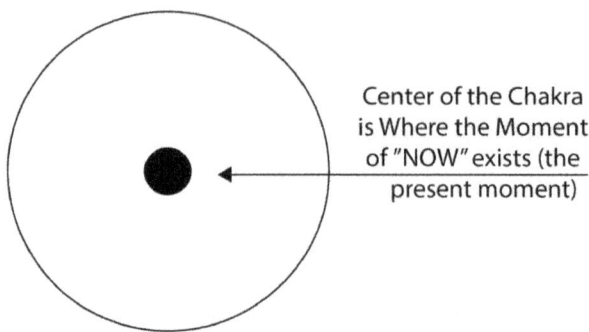

Front View of Chakra
with potential issues affecting the Moment of Now

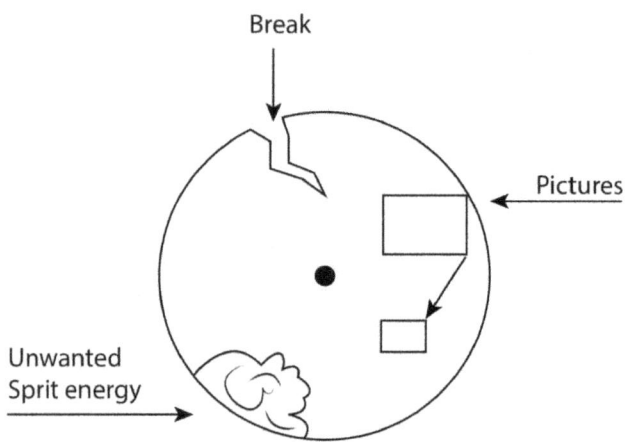

Practice:

Now that you've put up the circle, you've called in your guides, now start to run the earth energy up in counterclockwise motion from the outside of the circle to the inside of circle of the chakra.

Now imagine the healing Star Energy coming down into the chakra traveling in a clockwise motion. Stay there and keep dropping in healing energy until you feel the point of now is in the center of the chakra and is clearing.

Allow your guides to remove and clear any programming, beliefs, attachments, stuck energy that show up as pictures, implements, devices, cracks, cords, lower or murky energies that aren't yours. Some of the main issues that may show up are: family energy, controlling beings, religion, government, beliefs or experiences from this life or past lives. Look and see if everything looks aligned and in its proper place within your chakra. Is the moment of now in the center, are the lines and dots in their proper places?

If they are cracked or blocked or you feel or sense anything is not in alignment, follow the misaligned energy to the source, poke it and look what caused that to be out of balance. Now ask your guides to clear it and do the repair.

If you sense there is past life energy, or recurring patterns, attachment, or karma, you can ask your guides to end the karma in all time, directions, and dimensions.

Everything should feel clear and the energy should feel like it fits in snugly and securely. Your chakra will look balanced when the healing is right and complete.

This process takes as long as needed (some chakras might clear easily and others might take more time depending what's in there, illness, attachments, or you are coming to terms with releasing the energy etc.).

When you get a sense that the energy is cleared – pick up the pendulum and check the chakra again. If you get the signal your chakra is cleared and balanced (e.g. your pendulum is moving in a clockwise motion) you can now move on to the next chakra. If your pendulum signals it is not balanced – do the running exercises one more time, then check again.

When you are done repairing the chakra fill it with healing golden light. Feel your energy coming back to you. Your energy feels great in your body, you feel refreshed and revitalized, your energy coming home to you is a healing for you. You can end this practice by thanking your guides and yourself, clap your hands three times, and say "this healing is complete".

Healing with a Rose

The Rose is a high vibrational symbol and energy tool. When working with plant medicine the essence of the rose carries the highest frequency and is one of the most cherished and expensive pure oils. It is known as one of the symbols of Creator and carries the aroma of Source Creation.

Rose can also symbolize the principle of unconditional love, and unfolding, or opening as soul. We choose this as a tool and the intention we place in it is very powerful as it anchors the vibration for the healing. The Rose has been empowered by the Ancients that worked with this plant medicine and symbolic energy before us. All plants have certain divine healing, energies, and symbolic vibrations.

So, if you choose to work with the Rose, allow it to symbolize what you want it to symbolize. Know that if you choose to work with this symbol it will work for you 100%, ALWAYS! It is the way of the Creator.

Before you start any Spiritual work, it is my recommendation that you first say a prayer, call in your guides, and ground and run your energy.

What is the Issue?

The first step in this healing is to identify what you would like to work on or heal. For example: Why do I have a lack of money? What is causing me to feel so sluggish? Why am I accident prone? Why am I feeling anxiety etc.? Pick one thing to start with and be specific with your question. Remember, the question is about you and not someone else (at least for now, until I teach you how to do healings for others in my classes and advanced book)!

Now close your eyes and pretend there is a screen in front of you, connect a line from your third eye to the viewing screen, this helps you to look at yourself and be the observer. Now imagine a new line coming from your heart chakra to your third eye, this line connects your heart and your head to the experience. Then from the center of your heart chakra draw a new line to the screen. This allows you to observe yourself with love and compassion. You have made a trinity or triangle of spiritual observation.

Now imagine a rose on the screen. The rose that appears on your screen is holding the issue you would like healed within it, it is the vessel for this healing. Notice how the rose looks (color, shape, size, texture, open or closed), how it feels (it might present okay, but it feels something? Like off, or alone, or saggy, or dark). Notice if there are any cords, bugs, blemishes, squares, dots, pictures, tears, or discoloration (you may move the rose around to look at it from different angles so you can see what is going on) notice if the stem is grounded or connects to the bottom the screen.

Now that you've done a first pass and observed your rose, we are now going to do a technique using our spiritual hands. Pretend as if you are finger-painting or massaging and use your hands to reach into the screen and draw the stem down to the bottom of the screen and ground it to the bottom of the screen. You might feel something release, if it doesn't stay grounded take a moment to draw it down again, use your intention and guides to help you ground the energy of the rose to the bottom of the screen. Now run the Earth energy up the stem of the rose in a counterclockwise motion from the outside of the bud to the inside, let it run on an automatic grounding energy cycle.

Now drop down the star energy directly into the center of the bud of the rose, drop it in until you feel the star energy is fully connected to the center of the bud. This energy is moving in a clockwise direction from the inside of the bud to the outside.

Now with the energy on automatic cycle, we are going to first look to see if there are any squares on your rose anywhere, they can be what I call a "picture" or "snapshot" of something. If you'd like to see what that snapshot represents – tap on the square and allow it to open and show the scene from where and when the snapshot was taken (it could be from this lifetime or another). If you don't want to or have the sense that the picture is a belief that doesn't belong to you, move the square and place it into the center of the rose. Now, put all "pictures" and "snapshots" into the center of the rose.

Now look for any metal devices, shards, screw, bar, tool, anything foreign and ask your guides to pull it out and drop into the center of the rose.

Now look for or sense if there are any thought forms, or "beings" that are in the rose from past connections or people, that aren't of your own Source energy and give those "beings" and "thought forms" a place to go in the center of the rose. Watch all of them move into the center of the rose.

Now, look at the stem of the rose and notice if there are any "rings" on the stem. If you see any, count how many there are.

Rings on the stem of the rose represent "past life karma". There may be many or only a few or only one! Notice which ring is the "first" ring on the stem (it should be the ring that is closest to the bottom of the stem). This ring represents the first time you as a soul were learning about or dealing with this issue. If you'd like you can tap on this ring and look at what happened (this is optional) you don't have to know exactly what it is or when it happened to know it can be healed. If you'd like to review your past life – tap the ring and allow it to open. You can do this with each ring as those will show the times you have repeated this pattern throughout many lifetimes. You don't have to look at the rings or see what occurred – you can simply heal what is ready to be healed!

Now that you've noticed if there is any past life karma, you can heal this pattern by placing a radiant golden "Karma Completion Ring" at the top of the rose. Intend and feel all the "past life rings" magnetically drawn up to the golden ring and they are absorbed into the golden ring and now imagine the radiant ring as it is dropped into the center of the rose.

So now imagine a stick or a branch that represents the question, or issue you are healing. Now snap the stick and toss it into the center of the rose and the broken stick or twig symbolizes you "are done" with this issue in this lifetime!

Now we are looking for scrolls, you will find as many scrolls as you did rings on the stem. Break the scroll and tear the paper in half and drop them both into the rose.

This action ends all karma around this particular issue.

Now, you have two choices to make about your rose. You can delete the rose which means the energy starts to come out of your energy field, as the issues, imprints, past-life karma, foreign devices, etc. all leave your energy field, your original Source energy now returns to you. Or you can give the rose to your guides, this represents the guides taking it and transmuting it with you and for you.

Formally end the healing by thanking your guides and stating this "healing is complete". Clap your hand three-times, or play music, or wash your hands, whatever symbolizes closure.

WELL DONE – YOU'VE JUST GIVEN YOURSELF A HEALING!

Possible Effects of your Healing

As the energy continues to leave your body and energy field, you might yawn, you might have an immediate sense of lightness, joy, feeling great!

If you did a deep healing that also affected your physical body, you might experience any variety of detox symptoms (such as tiredness, tearing/crying, diarrhea, burping, emotional, or lightheadedness) as your body aligns to its new conditions after the healing. You might not have any side effects as each person is different, so just know if it is immediately after your healing, take it easy, rest, and allow your body to release and process. It is important to stay hydrated, so drink a lot of water, or enjoy some comforting herbal teas, and watch and feel as things start to change in your life as a result of this deep healing.

Any side-effects of spiritual healing might be 24-48 hours for symptoms of the healing to subside. Well done – you know you've done some excellent work!

May you be healed, because in truth – you already are.

- Sibyl Harmony

DREAMS

Everyone dreams when you sleep. You can go anywhere in the Universe in dreamtime, you aren't limited by physical restrictions such as health, money, or location.

Dreams are a way to connect with the unconscious mind, higher self, guides, messages, receive healing, see the future, ask questions, manifest, and receive visits from deceased loved ones.

There are several different ways that we dream and types of dreams. In some cultures, they believe that the dream plane (dreamtime) is more real than this one. Everything in a dream is you, or represents something you are working on or through, it may be prophetic, bringing you a message from pets or spirit guides, receiving healing, receiving a visit from deceased loved ones, or remembering past lives.

Some people have learned to change their dreams as in lucid dreaming. Although I do not change the dream while in the dream, I manifest where I want to go, or what I want to create or experience while still in waking state and prepare my Soul's journey before falling asleep. I do this by asking my guides and, or creating the symbol of a rose in a meditation and then send it out to the dream plane. I will guide through this exercise at the end of this chapter.

Anything you want to know you can ask to have a dream about. Like "please show me guidance about _____ fill in the blank". You can ask for a healing on the dream or astral plane. You can also ask for a visit from a deceased loved one, asking doesn't mean that you'll get it on that night. With deceased people best to make an appointment, because unlike angels and trained spirit guides deceased loved ones can't bi-locate and they may have a previous engagement or agreement about where they are supposed to be at the time.

I never tell God (Source, Universe, Goddess) what to do, but we can ask for the Divine will to be done.

Perhaps you can adapt the saying "this or something better." Your guides and angels will never control you or any situation. They know the divine plan, divine timing and work for the best of everyone involved.

What happens when we dream?

We have an astral cord, which is a soft, unobtrusive silver tube that is a natural part of our spirit body that connects to the third chakra (Solar Plexus) and tethers our spirit to our physical body in this life so we can adventure anywhere in this world or world's beyond and be able to find our way home, back to our current life and body.

How can you interpret your dreams?

In the back of this book I give you a dictionary of symbols so you can better understand and interpret your dreams, these symbols give you a starting point and a baseline to get you started – but the goal is to give you tools to help you trust and engage your own intuition. Many of the symbols may have different meanings to you, so trust yourself and your own inner connection and interpretation. For instance – if in your dream a pair of boots really stands out as a symbol for you and reminds you of your mother - trust that instinct and feel into what that symbol is sharing with you in the context of your dream. *Remember it is ALWAYS the FIRST intuitive hit that strikes your awareness that you want to pay attention to. Try not to overcomplicate it, or override your intuition with logic.

Types of dreams and examples of dreams where I received helpful messages from Spirit:

In one dream, I received strong guidance to pay off my home before the 2008 financial crash. During my dream, the bottom of my home literally fell out, I saw the floor was just gone. Upon waking I just knew I needed to pay my home off. To me the symbolism of the foundation of the house being gone, meant "the bottom is about to fall out" so because of my dream and understanding my own symbolic language, I was able to save my home.

In another dream I saw that my marriage was over. My marriage was in trouble, I tried counseling, healing, readings. One night I ask what would you have me do. I had a very clear dream of a brick wall. In other words, the brick wall meant "you hit the wall". Symbolically meaning you can't go past here. And on the wall it said in big letters SET HIM FREE.

Dreams can help you with real life situations and give crystal clear answers.

Dreams about healing. Many of the dreams I had when beginning my spiritual evolution were about animals acting strangely or being wounded. Wounded or sick animals behaving strangely can be unconscious parts of ourselves that need healing. Everything I mean EVERYTHING in the dream is you (there are some very few exceptions like visits from loved ones or nightmares). A nightmare can mean you're facing or clearing some fear or lower energies that may be affecting or you may be experiencing or remembering past life trauma that is being brought up for healing.

A visit from a deceased loved one. The night my Mother died she came in a dream and asked for forgiveness. She never took responsibility for anything much when she was alive. But the night she died she came to me. She was accompanied by grandmother angels with pink bathrobes. They all gave me a hug and she said she was sorry for everything she done to me. That was a visitation. When you have a visitation dream a part of you just knows it. Trust your heart.

Guidance from pets and living loved ones. Your pets are also very connected to the dreamworld and can act as guides or bring you messages and connect with you through your dreams. Susan lost her cat and she was worried it coming home but she felt he was okay, but he was gone and not responding to calls and search. The cat showed her in a dream that he would appear in her window when he was coming home. Two days later he came to her bedroom window to be brought back inside.

Prophetic Dreams foretelling the future. I had a prophetic dream that revealed to me a time in the future about the nature of humans and our potential to evolve and get better. I'll first share with you what was going on with me. I had formed a judgment about my friend's husband. This guy was a biker, he cheated on his wife a lovely woman, he cleaned out her bank accounts while chasing other women, and then he tried to rip me off by selling an investment that was worthless. Needless to say, I didn't like him and wanted nothing to do with him. I'd known this man for years and one night in my dreams I was shown the year 2680--. The earth was a beautiful place. There was no money. Everyone shared. Some lived in the hills and others in valleys. The earth was green and healthy again. The Goddess was back in balance. The air and water were clean and all the homes and buildings were built in harmony with the earth. I made my way to a big beautiful wooden community center that had beautiful harmonious energy. As I entered the main hall I looked up at large painting centered on the wall, and was totally shocked! The painting was of my friend's husband…that biker guy. I turned to a woman in the community center and I asked "why is that man's painting up there"? She looked at me indignantly, and then back to the painting and said, "he???... HE is our leader. He led us to freedom." I realized the lesson we are all avatars in the making. The lowest conman street cheating person could be your savior in the next life. That is the wisdom we can receive in our dreams as we evolve spiritually.

This dream helped me let go of judgments about others. I saw that my friend's husband had changed through many lifetimes and in the year of 2680, he had become a brave and respected man, a hero that helped everyone. When I ran into him in this life, I kept my distance but I didn't give any more attention or energy to judging him. I realized from my dream experience we are all just doing the best we can and are a spiritual work in progress.

Because what happens on the dream plane can then happen here much easier. Think of what you want before going to sleep. Of course we always say this or something better Gods will be done. That job you interview for. Ask to have second interview and dream that you get a communication and meeting your new employer on the dream astral plane. Or ask to meet someone really great a soul mate in a dream. Ask that you remember details and receive guidance about creating a new healthy happy relationship. Know that if you are asking the universe hears your request ven if you don't remember the dream. Have fun play with dream energy .As you practice you will learn more and become a skilled master.

How can you remember your dreams?

Some excellent ways to remember your dreams and to bring back messages you can simply have the intention that you will remember your dreams. Before you fall asleep say a prayer out aloud to your higher self *"help me to remember my dreams and messages that come tonight."*

A good practice is to place a paper or notebook and pen beside you on your bedside table. Unless you immediately write it down the second you wake up or take a moment to retell it to yourself or someone you will shift back into the physical and mental reality of you daily life and it will be gone.

Some people like to drink water before bed this will wake them in middle of the night with a better chance of remembering their dreams. I don't do that because I want to get solid nights rest.

I do however like to wake early morning am hours on a day when I'm off, I get up for a few minutes, no more than five to thirty minutes. Then if you go back to sleep you'll have dreams you can remember. I don't know why but it works great.

Also for some magical reason eating raw turnips will help you remember your dreams. It just works try it!

How to manifest and co-create using dreams.

If it is God, Goddess, or Higher Self's will, you can manifest it first in the spirit world/dream plane and then it will become part of our reality more quickly and easily and show up even better than what we imagined. Because whatever happens in the dream world, you are preparing for it to happens here – you are "calling it in". By asking for guidance and visualizing what we want or hope for before going to sleep we can begin to co-create with the divine.

Dream Rose Exercise: Create a Rose to send to the Dream World and Manifest your heart's desire.

For example – you would like to call in a new job.

First call in your guides, then visualize a rose of any color you like. This rose represents your new job. Now we are going to give the rose a healing. Visualize the rose's energetic field and see if there are any messages, cords, or tears, or pictures, or devices, see them – them simply ask your guides to heal whatever needs to be healed in your rose. See all of these things/issues being cleared and healed.

Once the rose is healed – imagine all of the things you do want and place them inside the center of the rose. If you want higher pay, a great boss who understands and listens to you, a relocation, an ethical company that values you, a company that uses sustainable practices and is Earth conscious, a schedule that works for you, insurance benefits, whatever you desire, speak it, imagine it, feel it, and place it in the center of your beautiful rose infusing it with good energy, light and unconditional love. Now bless this rose and hand it over to your guides to take to the dream world where it can manifest for you.

Congratulations you've just aligned your Soul and heart's desire to Divine Will in the dream state and be grateful when your new job arises with the right people, places, and circumstances for your Soul's growth at this time. Remember "This or something even better!" And always trust that the Universe is conspiring to bring you your desires in ways that may be unseen, and don't limit yourself and the potential by trying to control how your dreams come into being.

This is just one example of how you can use this Dream Rose exercise. Try this exercise to connect, manifest, and heal any area of your life in the dream state.

Dream on sweet Dreamer!

SUMMARY

Thank you for joining me on this brief journey and exploration through some of the foundations of self-healing. I hope you feel connected and empowered to the truth that you are Spirit, and spirit is energy, and you can heal yourself through energy medicine.

Everyone has their own healing journey, healing gifts, and way to heal themselves and the world. The more you explore and develop your own inner senses and are guided to learn and practice other modalities you will discover your healing agreements, and reveal your own healing path.

It has been one of the greatest gifts and best decisions of my life to seek out the healing tools and develop my own innate abilities. I've used these tools for decades to heal myself and others, and every day I am receiving even more divine guidance and healing energy to share with my clients and teach my students. When we are open as channels of healing energy, we can develop the ability to download and instantaneously heal ourselves and others. There is no limit to how energy can be used to create, manifest, and master energy. You can do this. This book gives you the basic foundations and practices to open your vehicle up to the healing frequencies that are available to you, so that you can co-create with spirit in amazing ways.

Nurturing our Soul's healing journey opens us up to who we really are as energetic beings. As we become aware of how energy works, we tap into our higher self and the spiritual realms of information, wisdom, and knowledge that are awakening within us.

Play, enjoy, explore, expand, and love yourself through this process of learning. You are stepping onto a most sacred path and using these tools you will be empowered through love to shift your vibration. As you cycle greater frequencies of love, healing, compassion, wisdom, connection, empathy, and peace you are helping to uplift and cleanse all of the energies and environments around you. You can affect the systems, environment, and health of the global and individual and social consciousness.

I look forward to connecting with you in one of my many courses, private sessions, workshops, and online classes.

May you manifest and be on our true-life path and aligned with your Soul's purpose. May you be healed because in truth, you already are.

Blessings and Joy,

Sibyl Harmony

Appendices - Prayers

I like praying with gratitude as if it has already happened. Giving thanks is a great way to pray.

Psalm 23

The lord is my Shepherd; I shall not want

Channeled Meaning: All enlightened beings address the same concept: There is divine being who is the Creator. This magnificent being you call God which might be a woman, the Bodhisattva, Great spirit, or Creator, takes care of all the needs of soul's who are on the journey back to the light. When these souls turn their attention and devotion to this being, they do not want for anything. The needs may change to what has true meaning and purpose. But they are taken care of.

He/She maketh me to lie down in green pastures

Channeled Meaning: The color green is reserved for the heart charka. It represents the heart center. In humans this center is the one that is most important. It is green light in the center of your chest. It is the center that we put emotional walls around when we are hurt.

When we connect with the creator and let creator open our heart center, we start to truly behave on a higher level, by opening this center we are truly in the green pasture and that contains all the ingredients of "empowered by love". We then can begin the process of awakening and evolving.

He She leadeth me beside still waters

Channeled Meaning: It is the acceptance of the heart center as the true source of wisdom. And the behavior related to states of higher consciousness, that one acquires the calmness and love the world is so hungry for. The mind gets the heart and soul into trouble when it is not at peace. It is at the moment of peace that the individual obtains mastery. It is the open heart that allows us to connect with Creator, divine beings, and open to our spiritual gifts of divination and healing. We are then ready to open our wings to our angelic nature and become who we truly are; the ascended Masters and highly evolved beings we already are.

He/ She restoreth my soul

Channeled Meaning: With the above in place, the soul is ready to undo all karmic debts. In this undoing, it prepares us for ascension and awakening. This means we are no longer bond to return life after life with the same people working on the karma over again. It means we are ready to forgive ourselves and others. We are truly free as we release karma.

He/She leadeth me of the path of righteousness for his her name sake

Channeled Meaning: When all karmic debts are released our soul is then free. On this planet this is called sainthood or the road to the Ascended Masters. It is the fifth dimension. The state in which one can command power and liquid light of the Great Central Sun. It is the opening of higher chakras six and seven. Six being the place of neutrality. Seven being the connection to your higher self. We are becoming angels and acceded masters that is why we came here to evolve and to be of service. We are transforming back to are original twelve strand DNA. This allows us to regain are ability's to spontaneously heal, the art of divination, and other supper natural gifts.

Yea, though I walk through the shadow of the valley of death, I will fear no evil

Channeled Meaning: The Earth is likened to the shadow of the valley of death. On Earth, the human consciousness is still evolving. It's considered by beings who dwell in the higher realms to be the *valley of shadow and illusions.*

Death is an illusion. These are pictures or beliefs we can chose to release. There is no death. It is a crossing over from one state of awareness to another.

On Earth, another illusion is that evil exists. Higher beings observe that our negativity and terror have been fed by millennia of human suffering through the power of the ego mind.

Therefore, when one walks on higher planes with God, the creator of all, evil and death are no longer feared or even real. When our consciousness transcends these illusions, there is no longer a need to retain these beliefs.

Since each person creates his or her own reality, though the power of the inner world, prayer, meditation, energy healing, once ego and fear are healed those quality's will no longer manifest on the earth plane or in the individuals life. You really have power though your thoughts, love more then you realize will become apparent to you.

Thou preparest a table before me in the presence of mine enemies

Channeled Meaning: The creator of all does not discriminate. God loves all souls with equal intensity of a father and mother. Therefore, regardless of what one does on the illusionary path, God does not punish, but prepares a feast table for all his children.

We are all chosen children of God. We may be given a vision of a chalice, a staff, crown, or prayer shawl, see a vision, receive dreams, feel the presence of the divine, hear guidance, know truth. We are all delivered from our weakness. It is only the ego that keeps us separate from the Sacred Father, Divine Mother, higher self, angels. God anointing of us with the mark of the savior. It is your choice whether you chose to accept or reject this initiation. We are then the enlightened, awakened being we already are manifest in physical form.

My cup runneth over

Channeled Meaning: *I am now open to receive.* This is when we know everything is energy and there is no lack. The universe is actually one of abundance not poverty. It is only our own consciousness that limits our perception of abundance.

Surely mercy and goodness shall follow me all the days of my life

Channeled Meaning: Comfort happiness and peace are the rewards of the children the light who choose to raise their consciousness. We are in harmony with nature and the natural rewards the earth shares with us.

And I will dwell in the house of the Lord

Channeled Meaning: When humans of earth learn to transcend their fears and limitations, they too will be able to explore other dimensions and dwell eternally in the knowingness of their own immortality.

The house of the Lord has many rooms. All souls are on the path back to the great central sun. In reality, all our journeys are one with the Creator.

Saint Teresa Avila

I say this prayer when I have lost something or asking for money:

Everything lost is found.

Everything stolen is returned.

Nothing disturbs me nothing frightens me.

All things pass away.

I have God and I find I lack for nothing.

Saint Francis Prayer:

Lord make me an instrument of your peace.

That I may sow love where there is hate

That where there is injury, I may bring pardon.

That where there is despair, I may bring hope.

That where there is darkness, I may bring light.

That where there is sadness, I may bring joy.

O divine master grant that I may not so much seek to be consoled as to console.

That I may seek to understand rather than be understood.

That I may love rather than to be loved.

For it is by pardoning that I am pardoned.

It is by dying that we awaken to eternal life.

Because our highest self is the will of the divine that we are happy joyous and free.

I will do the will of the divine.

May I do your will.

Take my hand, guide my steps walk me through this day.

Send me guidance and wisdom.

May I do your will always.

Another favorite.

May all people have a safe place to live.

Clean air, clean water, and enough healthy food.

May all animals be treated humanely and respected for their service.

May the environment be protected.

Thank you, Great Spirit.

Sufi Prayer

May the long time sun shine upon you.

All love surrounds you.

And the pure light lead you on.

DICTIONARY OF SYMBOLS

Having a dictionary of symbols for dreams, visions, mediumship, and everyday life can help you gain greater insight and transform the mundane into magical understanding. The sacred is not separate from you. *Everything has meaning.* Everything in front of you is part of the living dream called life that you are creating.

I invite you to have a conversation with life, and to add your own words, symbols and meanings to this dictionary as you go. Mark it up – put your own energy and insights into this document – it is just to get you started and on your way. This brief offering of symbols is in no way a complete dictionary of symbols. You can find a variety of books on the topics of symbols, symbolism, and dream dictionaries.

I have found (as with most things) the key is to listen, ask, and be present with what the Universe and Spirit are communicating to you. Look with your eyes and feel with your heart wide open and life will speak to you. You may receive visions or waking signs right in front of you, or in your mind's eye and your dreams. We are always receiving a downloads or broadcasts of love and guidance.

Interpretation starts with awareness. It can be as simple as seeing a certain kind of flower that catches your attention, noticing in that moment what you are thinking about or feeling and just being present. It might be that you always look at the clock when it's 1:11 or 3:33 or 4:11 – what do those numbers mean to you? What is Spirit wanting you to know? If an animal crosses your path or a bird swoops deliberately in front of you or your car, it is for you to decipher the meaning of that experience. Were they protecting you by catching your attention? Were they wanting you to research something or learn about their medicine in your life? Did the environment you were passing through at the very moment they appeared hold significance for you in some way? These are all messages for you. To learn more about the meaning of animals, I personally love the tool, **Medicine Cards** by Jamie Sams and David Carson.

Don't pass over your body's signals either. How you feel is also symbolic. You might get a chill, or a dizzy feeling, or feel warm and energized in the presence of a person, place, or object – these can be *aha* moments.

It is possible to hear symbols as well, bells, chimes, jackhammers, voices from a conversation you overheard while waiting for your coffee or lunch. These sounds can be ways to alert you, or possibly bring you confirmation of something you have been wanting to know or thinking upon.

When I see a dime on the ground or on the seat of the car - this is a sign for me that Mother energy is coming in. My Mother whom is on the other side always leaves dime when she's around. It's her way of saying "I care about you, I'm here". It can be your own personal association that gives meaning to whatever you see.

Practice meditating with paper and pen. Close your eyes, open your heart and ask your guides what the symbols that have been showing up mean to you. You can write down what you get in the pages below. Trust yourself. Start here to develop your own dictionary of symbols.

For those of you who are Mediums (you connect with deceased or dis-embodied Souls). This practice of collecting symbolic meanings is an amazing way to receive and interpret guidance and who the guidance may be coming from. If you would like to learn more about this sacred art, I teach entire classes and certifications on mediumship; it is fascinating and healing work.

Use this dictionary of symbols to get your creative imagination and intuition started.

I am here with you in divine space and you can reach me for support or help to develop your practice and learn more at any time ~ enjoy.

Blessings on your new or continued symbolic practice!

Sibyl,
xxoo

A

Activity:

1. **Bath:** cleaning is happening or needed.

2. **Clothing:** What role are you playing. What job did that person have.

3. **Digging:** How deep is it. The bottom is where you stop digging. Digging in stubborn, or hold your ground and dig in.

4. **Dragging:** Dragging around others stuff.

5. **Eating:** what foods do you need. Nourishing self.

6. _____

7. _____

8. _____

9. _____

Animals: Animals are the inner self what messages are they bringing you. Animals wounded what part of unconsciousness that needs healing. Dead animal what part of unconsciousness is dead or dying.

1. **Alligators:** Primal emotions out of control. Raw emotions. Out of balance emotions snapping at you, lower energies to clear.

2. **Ant:** Patience and joining groups work together. Collective unconscious.

3. **Ape:** is there a monkey on your back? Playing tricks? Big ape addiction. Small playful monkey: playful.

4. **Armadillo:** Boundaries.

5. **Bat:** Spiritual death shaman rebirth but first we are letting go what parts of us are dying or need to die so that we can be reborn.

6. **Beaver:** Trust protection tell truth. In distress betrayal.

7. **Bear:** Meditation. Rest. Feminine. Mama Bear. If a bear is chasing you or trying to get in where you are you need to look at, or confront your fears.

8. **Bee:** Get busy bees. Ancient Egypt. Immortality. Healing.

9. **Birds:** Spiritual and angels coming near. How is your spirit. Wounded bird spiritual wounding.

10. **Bobcat:** Silence is needed.

11. **Bug:** What's bugging you. Flu bug Parasites.

12. **Bull:** Male power. Bull in China shop watch out. Aggression. Assertiveness.

13. **Butterfly:** Change. Transformation. Stages. Progress. Beauty. What stage are transformation are you in beginning stage caterpillar, middle stage cocoon? The change has come when the butterfly is opening wings flying. Other meanings visit from loved one from the other side.

14. **Canadian Goose:** Mates for life, caring for loved one.

15. **Cat:** Independence. Feminine, Cats teach us how to treat them. Cat out of balance drug or alcohol addictions.

16. **Coyote:** Trickster in balance have fun with wacky energy. Out of balance look out for dishonesty and deceit.

17. **Crab:** Bottom feeder. Cancer Astrology. Shell, timid, shy, mother, protection.

18. **Crow:** Caw walk your talk. Unbalanced Get out of the gutter. Take the high road. Legal. Law. Contracts.

19. **Deer:** Heart. Gentleness. Intuition. Deer in the head lights frozen. Pay attention. Is it running downhill get away? Running uphill difficulty dealing deal with your fear.

20. **Dog:** Loyalty. Clan or family. Service. Friendship.

21. **Dolphin:** Joy. Playfulness for no reason, breath/breathing, fun.

22. **Dove:** Peace.

23. **Eagle:** Gods will. Bigger picture. Fly high close to the sun male beings of light. Out of balance or wounded you have forgotten your power or forgotten your vision.

24. **Elk:** Pace yourself honor, stamina in self. Spending time with your own gender. Out of balance don't stretch or force yourself.

25. **Fish:** Prosperity.

26. **Fly's bugs:** Lower astral form.

27. **Frog:** Cleaning physical, spiritually and energetically.

28. **Gorilla,** love, nurturing.

29. **Hawk:** Notice messages you're receiving. Wounded out of balance emotional over whelmed. Dead birds are spiritual death.

30. **Horse:** Power, sensitive

31. **Hummingbird:** Joy heart love.

32. **Lion:** Male king, female protecting young.

33. **Lizard:** Remembering dreams and dreaming in balance. Lower beings if scary.

34. **Mountain lion:** Leadership through humor and integrity.

35. **Mouse:** Details in balance. Out balance need to focus on bigger picture.

36. **Otter:** Playful

37. **Owl:** Sign of the psychic

38. **Pig:** Being selfish, or you need to put yourself first.

39. **Rabbit:** Don't call your fears to you.

40. **Raccoon:** Generous protector curiosity.

41. **Rat:** Intelligent. Pest.

42. **Seal:** playful energy's

43. **Shark;** Verbal attack. Watch out.

44. **Snake:** Kudilini energy. Awakening Sex and power. Out of lance confusion, lower energy ego beings controlling you

45. **Spider:** Creativity let go of resentments. Unbalanced pain from resentment from you or someone else.

46. **Squirrel:** Save gather energy. Out of balance frantic running in around, slow down clam yourself.

47. **Swan:** Mates for life. Soul mate or twin soul.

48. **Turtle:** Grounding abundance mother earth, slow down. Holding sacred earth energy.

49. _____

50. _____

51. _____

52. _____

53. _____

Arch Angels: Our powerful Angels here surrounding the earth. They are here to heal anyone that asks. The "el" at the end of their name means of God.

1. **Arch Angel Ariel:** Light pink. Watches over large cats wing creatures and large bodies of water. She worked closely with King Solomon to capture and put to work lower beings. She has the head of a lion.

2. **Arch Angel Azrael:** Is clear bright white: This powerful angel helps deceased souls cross over. She also helps with grief.

3. **Arch Angel Chamuel:** Is bright orange, he helps with finding soul mates and clearing lower ego energy.

4. **Arch Angel Gabriel:** Is bright sun yellow. She helps with child birth and children. She is also the angel to call when writing.

5. **Arch Angel Jermiel:** Is lavender. He helps with taking inventory of your life.

6. **Arch Angel Merton:** Is watermelon colors. He is two of the only Arch Angels that were ever human. He helps with healing with sacred geometry. Getting organized. Clearing lower energies. He helps teenagers or any one helps teens. He helps with A.D.H.D. (Attention dialed into higher dimensions). He works with depression or any mental conditions.

7. **Arch Angel Michael:** Moving healing.

8. **Arch Angel Rafael:** Is bright green and yellow gold. He helps with genital healing, children and pets.

9. _____

10. _____

11. _____

12. _____

Ascended Masters:

1. **Amaryllis:** Goddess of Spring.

2. **Amaterasu:** Japanese goddess of the Sun.

3. **Amen Bey:** A Fourth Ray Master. He works closely with Ptah and Archangel Michael. He is a protector.

4. **Angels:** Your guardian angels, also Arch angels here helping you. Guardian angels are here specifically for you personally. Each person usually has two. One more quiet and one more talkative. Angel wings you're an earth angel.

5. **Anubis:** Egyptian god of the underworld.

6. **Ares:** A Second Ray Cosmic Master. A warrior Master.

7. **Cha Ara:** A Fifth Ray Master.

8. **Chananda:** Chief of the Indian council of the Great White Brotherhood. A First Ray Master.

9. **Dom Ignacio:** Best known as the Ascended Master working with John of God in Brazil. He is a Third Ray Master.

10. **El Morya:** Chohan of the First Ray.

11. **Eros:** Also known as the god of Love.

12. **Freya:** Norse goddess of Love, Beauty, War, Magic, and Wisdom.

13. **Ganesh:** Hindu god of abundance and clearing the way.

14. **Gautama Buddha:** Lord of the World.

15. **Hathor:** An Egyptian Great Mother goddess. A Sixth Ray Master.

16. **Helios:** God of the Central Sun.

17. **Hilarion:** Chohan of the Fifth Ray.

18. **Hine-nui-te-po:** Maori goddess of the underworld.

19. **Inanna:** Sumerian goddess of love and war. A Fourth Ray Master.

20. **Isis:** Egyptian Goddess past life connections.

21. **Jesus:** Blue healing, forgiveness manifesting.

22. **Krishna:** A Cosmic Master.

23. **Kuan Yin:** Goddess of Mercy, not to be confused with White Tara. Many think they are the same Being, but their energies are very different. She is a Third Ray Master.

24. **Kuthumi:** The World Teacher and a master of the Second Ray.

25. **Lady Nada:** Lady Nada helps children and those who need inner child healing. She is a Sixth Ray Master.

26. **Lakshmi:** Goddess of Prosperity. She is a Third Ray Cosmic Master. Her aura blends from deep rose out to gold.

27. **Lao Tze:** A Chinese Ascended Master of the Second Ray.

28. **Lord Lanto:** Lord Lanto is Chohan of the Second Ray.

29. **Lord Ling (Moses)–** Lord Ling is a Chinese Ascended Master who was previously Moses.

30. **Ma'at:** Egyptian goddess of balance. A Third Ray Master.

31. **Maha Chohan:** Chohan of all the Eighth Ray.

32. **Maitreya:** The Cosmic Christ and planetary Buddha.

33. **Mary Magdalene:** A Third Ray Ascended Master.

34. **Melchizedek:** An Ascended Master of the First Ray.

35. **Metatron:** A cosmic angel of the First Ray.

36. **Mother Mary:** Light blue healing, children, women's issues.

37. **Omri-Tas:** A cosmic Master of the Violet Flame. A Seventh Ray Master.

38. **Osiris:** The Egyptian god of the afterlife. A First Ray Master.

39. **Pallas Athena:** The Sixth Ray goddess of Truth.

40. **Paul, the Venetian:** Chohan of the Third Ray.

41. **Portia:** Lady Ascended Master of the Sixth Ray for Justice.

42. **Ptah:** Fifth Ray Master, a warrior Master.

43. **Quan Yin:** Female Buddha Red and pink white, Compassion forgiveness selfless giving. Wish grating healing.

44. **Quetzalcoatl:** A Sixth Ray Master.

45. **Ra-Mun:** (Also spelt Ra-mu) An Ascended Master of the Seventh Ray and previous Chohan of the Seventh Ray.

46. **Sanat Kumara:** Lord of the World and the Ancient of Days.

47. **Serapis Bey:** Chohan of the Fourth Ray.

48. **Sitataptatra:** A goddess of the First Ray on the red aspect. She was the Ascended Master teacher of Gautama Buddha.

49. **St. Germain:** Chohan of the Seventh Ray.

50. **St. John the Baptist:** A First Ray Master

51. **Susan'oo:** Japanese god of summer storms, a Fifth Ray Master.

52. **Thomas Merton:** One of the newest Masters, a First Ray Master.

53. **Vesta:** Goddess of the home. A Third Ray Master.

54. **White Tara:** Goddess of Compassion and an Eighth Ray Master.

55. **Yogananda:** Paramahansa Yogananda

56. _____

57. _____

58. _____

59. _____

B

Body Parts

1. **Arms:** Giving right, receiving left.

2. **Back or Spine:** Support or lack thereof.

3. **Bladder:** Holding and releasing.

4. **Blood:** Life force.

5. **Bones:** Structure in life.

6. **Brain:** Thinking mind.

7. **Butt:** Power.

8. **Eyes:** Eyes are the windows to the soul. Third eye see more then the psychical world.

9. **Feet:** Following life path.

10. **Hair:** Power and or your thoughts.

11. **Hand to ear:** Did not get to say good bye. Holding hands close in life.

12. **Hands:** Together close relationship. Finger together very close. Waving hello or good bye. Reaching for you where you pulled apart. Are hands praying: prayers needed someone's praying for you.

13. **Heart:** Physical heart or love.

14. **Kidney:** Fear and grief.

15. **Knees:** Service.

16. **Legs and Hips:** Move us forward.

17. **Liver:** Anger.

18. **Lungs:** Grief

19. **Nose:** Value and reputation.

20. **Ovaries:** Creativity.

21. **Pineal gland:** Hormones, seat of spirituality.

22. **Sinus:** Telepathic channels.

23. **Skin:** Feeling safe and protection. Blood life force energy.

24. **Spleen:** Worries, sugar, immunity.

25. **Teeth:** Decisions, chewing over something, or life, assimilating life. How we break down things of life, decisions.

26. _____

27. _____

28. _____

29. _____

C

Colors

1. **Black:** Yang sacred darkness, illness death.

2. **Blue:** Healing, calm, water.

3. **Brown:** Calmness, earth, grounded. When murky abuse.

4. **Gold:** Highest vibration on earth plane.

5. **Gray:** Hazy, static, hiding.

6. **Green:** Growth, money, health, healing.

7. **Lavender:** Calming spiritual.

8. **Orange:** Masculine, Sun, action, control, sacral.

9. **Pink:** Female, love.

10. **Purple:** Deep purple religion, violet flame, higher-self,

11. **Red:** Hot, passion, energy vibrant, lucky, anger.

12. **Silver:** Moon, female, high vibration.

13. **Tan:** Calcite, practical, technical.

14. **White:** Bright high clear is purity innocence, birth, in. Dull or thick is toxin, deceased people, transmedia.

15. **Yellow:** Happiness bright and clear, family is it bright or chalky or dull.

D

Directions

1. **East:** Direction of what path to take. Spiritual strength, or challenges. Early life, youth, new beginnings.

2. **North:** Higher-self, life purpose inner teacher, warrior, chief, leadership.

3. **South:** Inner child, trust yourself and nurturing.

4. **West:** Goals internal solutions, later life, maturity.

5. _____

6. _____

7. _____

8. _____

E

Elements

1. **Cloud:** What shape is cloud. Not clear cloudy sky's cloudy energy. Before rain washing clean.

2. **Earth:** Grounding.

3. **Light:** Is it bright dull. Bright clean high vibration beings healing angels guides higher self-helping spirits or deceased people

4. **Moon::** Is it full or new. New moon beginnings for new projects. Full moon party, emotional, getting things done have fun. Moon is feminine energy. Soft receptive.

5. **Rain:** Water can be emotions and or wealth. cleansing, is it a genital nourishing rain. Or an emotional huge storm.

6. **Rainbow:** Opening to multidimensional, path guides came can descend to earth hope, joy. Or bi sexual. Leprechauns' gold.

7. **Rock:** What is hard in life. Lots of small rocks lots of little hard things in life. Large rock ground holding space. See crystal.

8. **Stars:** Star people other worldly, guiding light .to pray to Sirius.

9. **Sun:** In summer time. Masculine energy. Bold warm highest vibration of golden light.

10. **Water:** Emotions or prosperity. Turbulent water storms upset emotionalizing overwhelmed. Water moving towards your money coming. Muddy water confusion. Glass of water need to drink more water.

11. _____

12. _____

13. _____

14. _____

F

Flowers

1. **Basil:** Relationships muscles
2. **Cal-lily:** Helping with gender or bisexual issues
3. **Carnation:** Loving yourself.
4. **Clematis:** Poverty
5. **Clover, white:** Think of me
6. **Columbine:** Foolishness, Folly
7. **Daffodil:** Telepathic hearing spirit
8. **Daisy:** Smart keeping things simple, use your brain.
9. **Lavender:** healing calmness ending karma.

10. **Lilly's:** Higher thoughts

11. **Rose:** highest vibration sees colors; other flowers are not your energy. Or the emotional medicine needed.

12. **Rosemary:** Clearing lower astral beings

13. **Snap dragon:** Release anger

14. **Sun flower:** Male in balance sacred geometry Dandelion detox

15. **Sweet pea:** Be kind to self, forget me not past life healing

16. **Wisteria:** Nerve healing

17. **Valerian:** Readiness

18. **Violet:** Watchfulness, Modesty, Faithfulness

19. **Willow:** Be flexible.

20. **Yarrow:** Everlasting Love

21. **Zinnia:** Thoughts of absent friends, lasting affection

22. _____

23. _____

24. _____

25. _____

Food

1. **Beans:** Food sensitively, gas. Protein. Sustenance. Full of beans: gumption.

2. **Beer:** Favorite past time. Too much drinking

3. **Beets:** Liver cleaning grounding diet. Lower blood pressure

4. **Bread:** Stop eating wheat. Allergy. Gluten. Provided for. Full. Basics.

5. **Cake:** blue for male. Birthday coming. Pink for female birthday coming. If prices are missing birthday has passed. Each missing piece a week ago.

6. **Candy:** Problems with sugar. Sweet. Temptation.

7. **Christmas candy:** Fond memory of Christmas. Peppermint regrets or holiday depression.

8. **Diary:** Comfort food. What not to eat. See food.

9. **Doughnut:** Don't eat sweets. Needed something to make life sweet.

10. **Egg:** Beginning, New life.

11. **Grain:** Foods to avoid or food that is needed, no GMO.

12. **Grapes:** Abundance

13. **Green bean:** More veggies needed protein.

14. **Ice cream:** comfort food.

15. **Ice:** frozen feelings

16. **Lemon:** Do cleaning or body

17. **Lollipop:** Sugar issues or childhood merino.

18. **Nut:** Need for fun. Allergy. Sustenance. Preparation.

19. **Oregano:** Sanity. Antiviral

20. **Pie:** Over eating, what not to eat. Needed life to be sweet.

21. **Tea:** What to drink. Don't drink caffeine. Person that liked to drink tea. What herbal tea is needed for health?

22. **Walnut:** Intelligence look like a brain.

23. _____

24. _____

25. _____

26. _____

H

Holiday

1. **Beach:** Need to go to beach. Wanting vacation time to relax and go out in the sun.

2. **Camping:** The need to be resourceful, unplug, test resilience.

3. **Luxury:** Time for some comfort and treat yourself like Royalty.

4. **Business:** You can mix work and play if you learn how.

5. **Family:** Patience, closeness, forgiveness.

6. _____

7. _____

8. _____

9. _____

J

Jewelry

1. **Anklet** – Married or have a lover.

2. **Bracelet** – Friendship

3. **Crown** – Power, glory, immortality, royalty and sovereignty.

4. **Ring** – Infinity, Endless, Eternal

5. _____

6. _____

7. _____

8. _____

M

Magical Symbols

1. **Chalice:** Initiation. Reverence. (Silver, Gold, or Jeweled)

2. **Flying carpet:** Magical, rising spiritually to new levals, what is possible is now possible.

3. _____

4. _____

5. _____

6. _____

7. _____

8. _____

Miscellaneous

1. **Abdomen:** Place of power or abandonment issues.

2. **Ancient lands:** Past life.

3. **Army:** If in a mediumship session, it is what that person did in that life. Or is the warrior in you.

4. **Art:** creative part of self. What does it look like and or feel like when looking at a picture?

5. **Art:** What does the art look like feel like. Beliefs, collections, creativity.

6. **Bed:** Sleep issues, sex need rest.

7. **Birthday cake:** Satisfaction. Sweetness. If cut into birthday has passed, if not cut birthday is coming. Pink for girl blue for boy, yellow for unknown, non-gender conforming.

8. **Birthday gift:** Who just had a birthday. If gift is not opened, it represents the future. If gift is opened birthday has passed. Pink for female, blue for male, yellow for bisexual or neutral.

9. **Book:** Agreements. Writing or reading a book.

10. **Boots:** way to tell if man or woman. What kind of job did that person have or has. Work boots working person. Rain boots be prepared for wading through others emotion storms. Or be playful kids rain boots play in the rain.

11. **Break:** What's broken? An energy releases

12. **Brick wall:** You hit the wall. Don't can't go past this point. Let go.

13. **Bridge:** Was bridge crossed. If crossed they did what you are asking.

14. **Broom:** Clean out the old. Spring cleaning.

15. **Candle:** Bring light. Softness. Hope. Channeling.

16. **Child's wagon:** Childhood memories

17. **Church:** Person that was religious.

18. **Coins:** Messages from other side. Pennies from heaven. Family on the other side helping you with money. Dimes family on the other side calling. Mother. Calling

19. **Cup:** Drink or not drink this. See chalice.

20. **Dawn:** New beginning.

21. **Death:** Endings and beginnings there is no death. What part of you is dying so that you can grow spiritually.

22. **Deceased person:** Visit from that person. If person is distressed or fearful looking for help.

23. **Device:** Energy programming-what needs to be removed.

24. **Dish:** Something helping to nourish you. How big how much are you nourishing yourself.

25. **Doctor:** Pay attention to your health. Seek medical advice. Are you practicing to be a doctor?

26. **Door:** Opens to what. Is it old small big? Opening to other places or dimensions.

27. **Drain:** What needs to be drained. Are you being drained? Is drain clogged.

28. **Drunk and drinking:** Drunk and drinking.

29. **Egypt:** Past life.

30. **Fair/Carnival:** Fun, childhood, games.

31. **Famous person:** What does that person represent to you.

32. **Fearful dreams and visions:** Need for prayer, blessings and healing. These are lower energies and fear. Don't feed fear by being fearful. Illusions only God and love are real.

33. **Fence:** Are you on the fence. Is a fence separating you from somethings? Boundary

34. **Fireman:** To the rescue. Or someone that came to rescue.

35. **Flag:** Vet, patriot.

36. **Gift:** A gift is coming. What's to give you a gift. A holiday just happened if open, will happen if not opened. See birthday

37. **Grave:** Deceased person contacting you. What part of you is dead or dying.

38. **Hat:** What role are you playing. Nurse hat sing of helpful person or medical career.

39. **Haunted house:** need to release negative energy's and fears. Healing is needed.

40. **Hospital:** Need medical help. Emergency, surgery.

41. **Hotel:** Part of business self.

42. **House:** symbol of you. Basement lower chakras. Middle middle chakras, Upper floors higher self or higher chakras. What shape is your house in. Parts of you you where unconscious of. Who is your space?

43. **Jail:** What part of your life is not free.

44. **Judge:** Being judged. Being judgmental. Fair Judge is justice will be done.

45. **Jungle:** What is wild inside you. Discover new or wild parts of self.

46. **Kill:** To kill part of self.

47. **King:** Leader older emotionally available. Present for a marriage earned his kingdom.

48. **Kite:** Soaring high.

49. **Knight:** Coming to rescue. Likes adventure. Not ready to settle down.

50. **Lemuria:** Past life

51. **Leprechauns:** Elemental being bringing luck.

52. **Letter:** Agreement, wills, important legal or personal messages.

53. **Love:** Falling in love. Love is being sent.

54. **Medication:** Person was on medication. What is needed. What is not working side effects and addictions.

55. **Metal devise:** Energy programmed that needs to be removed energetically.

56. **Money:** Energy not bad or good.

57. **Navy:** Person was in the Navy.

58. **Numb:** Unable to process something. No feeling or detached.

59. **Nun:** Past life religious. Religious guilt Nurse: Helping healing. what that person did for job.

60. **Nurse:** Helpful person. Therapy. Support. You need nurturing or support.

61. **Page:** Too young for serious relationship. Young make that is childlike learning.

62. **Paper:** Write make agreements will, messages. Write.

63. **Path:** Path in middle of road going towards sun on the right path and life purpose. Path going off to right male, money monetary, physical distractions. Off to left emotional or female distraction. What is taking you off your life purpose or path.

64. **Pen or pencil:** Write

65. **Phone:** Call someone. Call 911 you need help call for help. Communication issues who do you need to communicate with.

66. **Poo:** Clean up your act. Have you steeped in it?

67. **Pool:** Water represents money and or emotions. Abundance clam water is clam emotions. What area is the water in regrade to Feng Shui. See Fung Shui Bagua.

68. **Prince:** Available for relationship. Will be working and focused on building kingdom.

69. **Princess:** Young woman child baring years. Present for relationship.

70. **Pyramid:** Energy power shape, ancient Atlantis Egypt life.

71. **Queen:** Older women, mature, good relationship.

72. **Rape:** Violence, to consume another and take away their power.

73. **Relative:** Male or female side of you like that person. Or a visit from that person.

74. **Rug:** Decor, what is padded made comfortable, style, luxury.

75. **Sex:** Bond with in one's self. Blending of male female energy's within bring spiritual grow and well-being. Energy connection with person or spirits having sex with.

76. **Skunk:** Respect yourself. Unbalanced do not expose feelings inappropriate behavior, sober up.

77. **Smoke:** Where there smoke theirs fire. Smoke screen what hiding in the smoke.

78. **Snap fingers:** Happens quickly.

79. **Square space in Aura or chakra:** Picture. Beliefs form event, past life or another person.

80. **Text:** communication who do you need to communicate with.

81. **Toy:** Childhood memories. Message to play more.

82. **Umbrella:** Protection shield, shield yourself.

83. **Wall:** Hit the wall end of path. C liming wall getting over something. Crumbling wall what falling apart.

84. **Wheelbarrow:** hauling around unfinished or someone else business.

85. **Will (legal document):** What do you really desire? What is your legacy? Your past life contracts.

86. **Window:** other side watching over you. Different way of looking at something. You can see.

87. _____

88. _____

89. _____

90. _____

Mythical Creatures

1. **Angel wings:** Are feathered like a large bird wing, comfort, protection, what do Angel wings mean to you?

2. **Elf:** Magical being.

3. **Dragon:** Supernatural power, wisdom, strength, and hidden knowledge

4. **Griffin:** Strength and military courage and leadership.

5. **Pegasus:** Tamed by noble and kind-hearted horsemen, inspiration to poets, philosophers, and artists.

6. **Phoenix:** Surviving out of the ashes to glory.

7. **Unicorn:** Christ and Mother Mary themselves

8. _____

9. _____

10. _____

11. _____

N

Numbers

1. 0: God or goddess

2. 1: One is thoughts pay attention to thoughts. Your thoughts will manifest.

3. 2: Have faith. Believe faith is with you.

4. 3: Ascended Master are with you Jesus, Mother Mary, Buddha, Qun Yin, Krishna seeing 333

5. 4: Angels and Arch angels are here and helping you. Seeing 4

6. 5: Change has come or is imminent.

7. 6: Don't worry about the physical.

8. 7: Very auspicious.

9. 8: Never ending eternity. Money coming. Healing.

10. 9: Service.

11. 10: Thoughts and God.

12. 11: Thoughts are manifesting think of what you want. Right before the change

13. 12: End time of change. It is done.

14. 13: Lucky sing of Goddess.

15. 411: Information for you.

16. **911:** Emergency pray for help.

17. _____

88. _____

19. _____

20. _____

<u>P</u>

<u>Person</u>

1. **Boy:** Young male part of you.

2. **Child:** Young part of self. Or visit from a child you knew.

3. **Dad:** Your father visiting. Part of you like Father or Fathering self.

4. **Female:** left side, intuition, mother, sister, girlfriend, the feminine part of yourself.

5. **Girl:** Young part of female self.

6. _____

7. _____

8. _____

9. _____

Planets

1. **Jupiter:** Belief, Travel, Expansion

2. **Mars:** Energy, Vigor, Initiative

3. **Mercury:** Intellect, Communication, Understanding

4. **Neptune:** Intuition, Dreams, Psyche

5. **Pluto:** Rebirth, Transformation, Hidden Power

6. **Saturn:** Control, Determined, Fixation

7. **Uranus:** Change, Invention, Revolution

8. **Venus:** Beauty, Harmony, Attraction

Plants

1. **Basil:** herb for helping relationship harmony.

2. **Cactus:** Protection it has thorns.

3. **Calla Lilly:** Gay bisexual.

4. **Grass:** Healing grounding. Is it dry and dying not fertile ground? What is the grounding look like? Ground yourself to the earth.

5. **Herbs:** Helpful medicine suggestions.

6. **Tree:** Grounding Pine structure bones release blame. Eucalyptus: Breath heart, emotion. Oak: Strength. Olive: peace

S

Sports

1. **Ball:** Most powerful shape. Playing sports having fun.

2. **Baseball:** Sports. Size of something. Hardness.

3. **Card:** special occasions is or just happened. Sentimental memories

4. **Football:** Games rough sport.

5. **Game:** playing a game.

6. _____

7. _____

8. _____

9. _____

T

Tools & Weapons

1. **Ax or Axe:** Implement Psychic attack.

2. **Gun:** Psychic attack.

3. **Knife:** Psychic attack.

4. **Sword:** Psychic attack. Or comrades in arms strongest bond.

5. **Tank:** Weapon of war.

Transportation

1. **Boat:** Spiritual journey. What type of boat is it? Is it fast speed boat? Large sailing ship? Small little canoe.

2. **Bus:** Attempt to fit in the crowd.

3. **Car:** Physical body. Whom in the driver seat. Only you should be driving your car. Who's in control of your body. Car going uphill health improving. Car going straight or flat things staying the same. Car going downhill change what you're doing, runaway health is getting worse or out of control.

4. **Elevator:** Next Chapter of your life

5. **Flying:** Motivation, its role being to push you forward until you achieve your goal.

6. **Plane:** high aims, spiritual aspiration and sexual arousal.

7. **Train:** Extraordinary bundle of relations.

8. **Scooter:** Breezing through a situation or problem.

9. **Stairs:** Ascent, Descent, Climb, Step.

10. **Walking:** Intrinsic need to be free, seeking an initiating experience, of change.

11. _____

12. _____

13. ───────────────────────────────

14. ───────────────────────────────

15. ───────────────────────────────

ABOUT THE AUTHOR

Sibyl Harmony is a Teacher, Master Healer, Mystic Medium, and nondenominational Pastoral Counselor. Embodying Cherokee, Egyptian Gnostic, and Temples of Isis spiritual healing lineages Sibyl Harmony has been here in divine service, reading, teaching, and healing for over 25 years.

In the ancient times of the Goddess, "Sibyls" were Prophets, Healers, Therapists, and Pastors who served their communities.

Receiving communications from the divine and the elemental realms since she was a child, Sibyl has healed the source of her chronic fatigue, thyroid, depression, and other health issues using energetic medicine. She has traveled the world to study with shamans and now shares her teachings and wisdom with you.

WORK WITH SIBYL

Book Private Sessions

PSYCHIC TAROT & MEDIUMSHIP

HEALING

DREAM INTERPRETATION

RELATIONSHIP READINGS

LIFE PURPOSE, CAREER & PROSPERITY

GROUP READINGS

Workshops, Classes & Certificate Courses

THE GATEWAY – YOUR ENERGY ANATOMY

DIVINE GUIDANCE

PSYCHIC DEVELOPMENT & VIBRATIONAL HEALING

PAST LIFE REGRESSION & DREAMS

HOW TO WORK WITH THE GODDESS

TO BOOK A SESSION OR ATTEND A WORKSHOP VISIT:

SIBYLHARMONY.COM

HARMONYSIBYL@GMAIL.COM

FUTURE TITLES FROM SIBYL HARMONY

The Time of the Goddess

Ishtar. She is here to teach us that the Goddess is every woman, how to reconnect us with our intuitive abilities, how to remember seeing the aura, and how to regain our power, connect with the Earth and align ourselves with nature the planet and the stars.

Problem "Solved", So Loved, Soul Loved.

Sibyl the Sybil Sisterhood – Temple Time

Advanced Energy Healing

Join Sibyl as she guides you through the inner realms and how to access and shift stuck, blocked, ancestral, and attachment energy. Continue your development from Self-healing to Practitioner of Healing.

PRAISE FOR SIBYL HARMONY

"I am so thankful to Sibyl for the guidance and healing that she has given me over the years. Sibyl is highly skilled in working with energy—she has helped me overcome relationship issues, physical injuries and illnesses, and substance abuse. What I love most about Sibyl is that she is a loving, nurturing being who cares about helping people live better lives. I highly recommend Sibyl to anyone who is reading this. She will help you change your life."

~ Nick S., Attorney

Sybil is a treasure of a healer. The soul-learnings and beautiful symbolic-based wisdom she has channeled over the years continues to support me. She also gives distance healings to my family and I can see positive transformations in them as well.

~Amy T.

I feel as if my cosmic heart is finally open and expanding as a result of my angels' and guides' messages from Sibyl's reading and healing.

~Tracy C., healer, Canada

Sonoma Healing Press

We hope you've enjoyed **White Rainbows by Sibyl Harmony.**

Sonoma, CA | Nevada City, CA | Phoenix, AZ

www.SonomaHealingPress.com

+ 1 (707) 309.1393

www.ingramcontent.com/pod-product-compliance
Lightning Source LLC
Chambersburg PA
CBHW061200070526
44579CB00009B/76